In at the Dee

Teachers working in post-compulsory education are recognised as being subject to a particularly acute set of pressures and challenges. These can include highly diverse and sometimes challenging student groups, trying to manage a complex curriculum which changes regularly and rapidly, and having to respond to the intense demands of inspection, quality assurance regimes and major government policies.

Now in its second edition, the highly regarded *In at the Deep End: A survival guide for teachers in post-compulsory education* will help you to manage the varied demands of teaching in PCE more effectively by offering friendly, professional advice and a range of teaching and learning activities which will help you become an effective, confident, committed and reflective teacher.

With a range of strategies, activities and spaces to reflect, this positive and practical 'survival guide' provides advice on:

- meeting initial challenges, working positively with your students and handling challenging behaviour;
- accessing support, working with your local colleagues and a greater community of practice;
- using straightforward techniques to help you manage pressure and conflict;
- supporting skills for life, key skills and functional skills;
- making positive use of Information and Communications Technology to support learning;
- teaching your specialist subject;
- managing inspections, developing as a leader and becoming a 'Reflective Practitioner'.

Lively and engaging, and built from the experience of many teachers across the last 30 years, this book will help all teachers overcome everyday problems and pressures to keep their 'heads above water', and become efficient, skilled professionals in the post-compulsory education workforce.

Jim Crawley is Programme Leader of Lifelong Learning at Bath Spa University.

In at the Deep End

A survival guide for teachers in post-compulsory education

Second edition

Jim Crawley

 Routledge
Taylor & Francis Group

LONDON AND NEW YORK

First edition published 2005 by David Fulton

This edition published 2011
by Routledge
2 Park Square, Milton Park, Abingdon, Oxon, OX14 4RN

Simultaneously published in the USA and Canada
by Routledge
711 Third Avenue, New York, NY 10017, USA

Routledge is an imprint of the Taylor & Francis Group, an informa business

© 2011 Jim Crawley

Typeset in Bembo by Prepress Projects Ltd, Perth, UK

British Library Cataloguing in Publication Data
A catalogue record for this book is available from the British Library

Library of Congress Cataloging-in-Publication Data
Crawley, Jim.
In at the deep end: a survival guide for teachers in post-compulsory education/
by Jim Crawley. — 2nd ed.
p. cm.
Includes bibliographical references and index.
1. Teaching—Great Britain. 2. Post-compulsory education—Great Britain. I. Title.
LC1039.8.G7C73 2011
373.11′00941—dc22
2010006421

ISBN10: 0-415-49988-7 (hbk)
ISBN10: 0-415-49989-5 (pbk)
ISBN10: 0-203-84564-1 (ebk)

ISBN13: 978-0-415-49988-0 (hbk)
ISBN13: 978-0-415-49989-7 (pbk)
ISBN13: 978-0-203-84564-6 (ebk)

To Jan, who has kindly travelled from the magical planet Janice to be my beautiful, wise wife, and to Dan, Tim and Rosi, our lovely children, and my first granddaughter, Sophie, who is a delight.

Life has thrown some interesting things in our direction since the first edition of this book was published, but Jan and the children, and the rest of my family, continue to help me remain mostly cheerful, positive and able to come out the end of it all with a smile.

Contents

Preface

Since the first edition of this book came out in 2005, some major changes have taken place in the world and in post-compulsory education (PCE). There have been three name changes in the department which is responsible for PCE since then, the 'official name' of the sector has changed at least twice, and there will be more changes after the general election which took place in May 2010. A new range of teaching qualifications has been introduced, not without pain, and many more teachers have started the process which will end in them gaining the new Qualified Teacher (Learning and Skills) or Associate Teacher (Learning and Skills) status. The Institute for Learning, the professional body for the sector, has a membership of over 200,000 at the start of 2010.

Oh and by the way, in case you didn't know, there is a global recession taking place, and education is expecting deep cuts and efficiency savings over the next few years!

Post-compulsory education is used to frequent, at times, illogical and counterproductive change, so we should probably not be surprised, but I feel the next few years will be particularly challenging. A 'survival guide' such as this book could become even more useful.

I've now worked in PCE for nearly 35 years and, since the first teaching work I did as a supervisor on a late 1970s job creation scheme, much has changed beyond all recognition, and yet some things have remained strangely the same. Post-compulsory education has always sat somewhat uncomfortably between school and higher education, and exerts less power and influence. In fact it often appears to exert virtually no power or influence at all. Post-compulsory education has always worked with disadvantaged members of the community, and readily embraced diversity amongst its students and staff. The last 10–15 years of the period I worked in a further education (FE) college saw the working situation for teachers deteriorate into what can only be described as thinly veiled chaos, and teaching staff in PCE now get paid some 20 per cent less than their colleagues in schools. Sometimes the constant change has seemed more like a cunning plan to keep us all under control by ensuring we are so absurdly busy that rebellion is out of the question (we're all far too tired and run down!).

One thing does continue to keep us all going, even in darker times. Despite all the changes, reorganisations and initiatives, once we are teaching and supporting our students, what goes on essentially remains constant. As a teacher, or as one of a team of teachers, we work really hard to help our students to learn, and many of them actually do.

Many people describe PCE as a sector which is complicated, difficult to define, and equally difficult to develop as a coherent entity, and I'm not going to disagree with that. What does, however, bind the sector together in the most meaningful way is the shared enterprise of all the teachers who are working together to improve the life chances of their students.

This second edition of the book is not dramatically changed, but it has been updated, tweaked and I hope improved so that it can:

- encourage teachers in PCE to feel part of a shared and valued community;
- help some teachers to do their job better, and enjoy it more;
- help more members of the community to learn new things.

If it does, it will have been well worth writing.

Who is this book for?

The main audience will be new teachers to PCE, probably in the early stages of their careers (perhaps the first three years). A significant proportion will be working towards completing some form of initial teacher training during those first years. This book will provide both practical support and guidance for their day-to-day teaching, and strategies, activities and spaces to reflect which will be useful on all of the current initial teacher training courses such as Preparing to Teach in the Lifelong Learning Sector (PTLLS), Certificate to Teach in the Lifelong Learning Sector (CTLLS) and Diploma to Teach in the Lifelong Learning Sector (DTLLS). It is also relevant for all staff teaching and supporting learning (whether they are new or experienced) in the growing PCE sector. Many of the themes and topics are universal to all teachers, so it should also be helpful if you are teaching in a school or university, and much should be as relevant outside the UK as inside.

The book takes an approach to content which is consciously eclectic, as there are many ideas, models, activities and examples out there which can be useful for teachers in PCE. It unashamedly draws on many sources, not all of which necessarily agree with each other. Theory and academic thinking are not forgotten, and are drawn in to support the development of practice, and to make that practice more meaningful. All of the content is focussed on the book's central objective, which is to help you survive and develop as an effective, confident, committed and reflective teacher. The influences and ideas therefore may to some degree be mixed, but the message remains the same. That message is that teaching is an exceptionally important profession, and that doing it well is a goal we should all strive for together.

Much of what is in the book would also give managers in PCE a clearer insight into what their teaching staff really experience on a day-to-day basis, and how they try to manage some of the pressures they are under. It would be a practical and straightforward way for a manager to get into the world of the teacher, and could be a real help for managers who genuinely want to support their staff, improve quality, and get better results.

If you enjoy the book, take a look at my web site, 'Itslife', which is intended to provide information and links to other web sites for those who are working in PCE. You can find it at http://www.itslifejimbutnotasweknowit.org.uk

Acknowledgements

Thanks to my colleagues Caroline Harvey and Rose Smeeton for their work with me in PCE. They are both excellent teachers, and have demonstrated considerable survival skills themselves in many years of experience within the sector. They are also an important part of the group of colleagues with whom I have regularly worked during my career in PCE, and who have helped me to get better at what I do.

Special thanks to my wife Jan, who doesn't work in education, but being wise, and working in community development, has offered a perspective from outside the education system, which has been invaluable.

Welcome to post-compulsory education (PCE)

1

Introduction

This chapter will introduce the upbeat and positive rationale behind the book, which is essentially that teaching in the post-compulsory sector, although at times challenging, exhausting and frustrating, is also often a hugely enjoyable and rewarding area of work, which makes a contribution to civil society like no other. Guidance on how the book can work for you best, and how it is structured to provide variety and activity is also included, and a 'call to arms' to send you all on your way looking forward to your teaching and of course to the rest of the book!

An introduction to the deep end

As a teacher you bring your own unique life experience, personality and skills with you to the job of teaching, and you will often need to draw deeply on them in the rich and varied world which is PCE. In addition to preparing and carrying out your teaching in a rapidly changing and developing curriculum you will encounter a maze of bureaucracy and administration. While you are trying to prepare for inspection, working towards the latest quality standard or benchmark, and expecting your next internal classroom observation, there are some essential personal qualities which will keep you going, and help you survive as a working professional. They are *enthusiasm*, *energy*, *resourcefulness* and *resilience*, and perhaps the most indispensable of all, and at times the single most important, a *sense of humour*. If you don't possess most of these qualities in abundance at the start of your teaching career, you may want to take a careful breath, and consider a more peaceful life! Believe me, there will be times when laughing is the only possible reaction to some of the situations you will encounter.

Starting work as a teacher can be complicated and confusing, as there is much to learn, and never enough time to learn it. Many of the 'official' aspects of being a new teacher can seem almost irrelevant as you struggle to plan and organise your timetable, which contains more than 20 hours of teaching and many other related tasks and activities. It can feel very much like being 'in at the deep end' and at times sinking could be much more straightforward than swimming.

There are however many things which can help over the early stages of being a teacher, including help from other colleagues, support from the culture and habits of your organisation, and learning through your own successes and mistakes. The trouble is that, by the time you have learnt all these things, you have often already been teaching for one or two years. Then of course they all change again! You will have often thought 'If only I'd known that when I started'. This book has used the benefits of a considerable pool of experience of the author and many friends and teaching colleagues to try to provide you with some of those answers, hints and tips in advance, or at least earlier than you would get them if you relied on just learning from your own experience.

As we will explore in more detail later in the book,

learning is something essential in human life.

Foley (2004), when discussing adult learning, puts this nicely:

As . . . David Kolb (1984) has noted learning is human beings' primary mode of adaptation: if we don't learn, we may not survive, and we certainly don't prosper. All human activity has a learning dimension. People learn informally and formally, in many different settings; in workplaces, in families, through leisure activities, through community activities, and in political action.

(Foley 2004: 4)

Although this comment is about adult learning, and PCE works with students as young as 14, it resonates strongly within the overall approach of this book. Even though the implication from such a view is that teachers and teaching are a relatively small part of the wide world of learning, it is a crucial part, which in many cases and situations can be the key to positive and successful learning.

At the heart of this book is therefore one of the most positive aspirations which any career can possibly have. As you strive to combine the 'essential you' and those other qualities with important skills, understandings and approaches relating to teaching and learning, you genuinely are on one of life's most important, yet often under-rated missions, which is to help other people to learn.

You may or may not feel that education can change the world, but there is no doubt that at some stage, and if you're both lucky and good at your job, you will often help to change someone else's world and life for the better.

Never underestimate the power of learning.

As a teacher, what will drive you on is the knowledge that learning can still transform, and can really make a difference. Let's face it, if that isn't worth trying to do as well as you can, what is?

Good luck with the journey!

Making the book work for you

There is an intentional progression through the book, which shadows the journey of the teachers reading it. In the early chapters you will cover topics and themes which will be most relevant to new teachers, at the time when they feel immersed in the 'deep end'. We will then progress on to more detail about areas of work which you will take on as you gain more experience, and the later sections focus on the expected development of a more confident mastery of the craft of teaching. The structure is designed to help your own career pathway to move in the same direction. Navigation through the book is clear and straightforward with generally short chapters, each of which starts with a summary of content. Themes covered include:

- basic principles and practicalities of teaching and learning;
- management and survival skills which will help your day-to-day work;
- developing support networks;
- actively promoting equality and diversity through your teaching;
- extending your own specialist subject;
- working with learning technology;
- getting the best from mentoring;
- being 'actively critical';
- getting involved in research and development;
- managing your managers.

A glossary of relevant terms appears at the end, whilst a bibliography is included on a chapter-by-chapter basis. The book is not referenced directly to national standards, and use is not made of learning objectives for chapters or activities as is often the case with other books in the field. This is partly because national standards for PCE tend to change frequently, whilst many key concepts and practices involved in teaching remain surprisingly stable, but mainly because this book is much more concerned with accessibility and a developmental approach than closely mapping to particular standards. Much of the content will relate directly to teaching standards in terms of topics, professional knowledge, values and the actual skills involved, but it is a more holistic notion of teaching which underpins the whole book, as will be evident from the start. National standards do have some benefits, however, and defining some of the key areas associated with teaching is one of them.

The most recent set of national standards were published by Lifelong Learning UK in 2006. They include the following statement about the 'key purpose' of Teaching:

Teachers in the lifelong learning sector value all learners individually and equally. They are committed to lifelong learning and professional development and strive for continuous improvement through reflective practice.

The key purpose of the teacher is to create effective and stimulating opportunities for learning through high quality teaching that enables the development and progression of all learners.

(Lifelong Learning UK 2006: 2)

The book does certainly take account of the current set of national standards and ongoing reforms of teacher education, but overall we agree with Nasta's statement that:

> Agreeing standards should be seen as very much the beginning rather than the end of reform.
>
> (Nasta 2007: 15).

Standards come and go, but we want to provide practical advice and support which will be helpful for years.

Thinking points and strategies for survival

One key feature of the book is the use of 'Thinking Points'. These provide focussed, accessible and realistic activities, examples, scenarios and reflections, or 'mini tasks', which create variety, and something of a pause for thought and reflection. They may take the reader away from the text to think about or do something directly related to their practice, or provide a chance to try out something new and reflect on it before moving on to the next section or chapter. They are also activities which can be adapted for use in a wide range of teaching situations, so should provide you with ready-made teaching resources.

Food for thought is interesting, but won't help you survive on its own, so we also suggest ways you could act on your reflections. 'Strategies for Survival' will therefore often follow 'Thinking Points', so that you can make use of them on the journey out of the deep end.

The index

The index to the book is organised to ensure you can find content easily on key topics such as learning, planning, supporting students, and will provide a different route through the book if that suits you better.

The vision

What can often seem like a fragmented, poor-quality, badly managed and indeed chaotic sector does actually achieve amazing results for and with many of its students. This is often despite as difficult and challenging circumstances as you could possibly imagine for the students. The people who are at the heart of the many successes in PCE are of course the students themselves, but the key professionals, who more than anyone else deserve a share of that success, are the teachers. This book is intended to help teachers in PCE extend that success into the future, and help the sector to get the recognition it deserves.

References

Foley, G. (ed.) (2004) *Dimensions of Learning: Adult Education and Training in a Global Era*. Maidenhead: Open University Press.

Kolb, D. (1984) *Experiential Learning: Experience as the Source of Learning and Development*. Englewood Cliffs, NJ: Prentice-Hall.

Lifelong Learning UK (2006) *Professional Standards for Teachers, Tutors and Trainers in the Lifelong Learning Sector*. London: LLUK.

Nasta, A. (2007) Translating national standards into practice for the initial training of Further Education (FE) teachers in England. *Research in Post-Compulsory Education*, 12 (1): 1–17.

2

What is post-compulsory education?

Teaching takes place in a rapidly changing world, and this chapter introduces that context of rapid change in the world around us, and how as teachers you can positively encounter and manage that change as part of your work. A description of just what we mean by post-compulsory education in this book follows, with examples of the kind of teaching situations you may find yourself encountering. The chapter closes by outlining the diversity of the student body in PCE, by which time you should have a deeper understanding of the nature of the sector, and aspects of your teaching role within it.

The changing world of post-compulsory education

Life in the twenty-first century will continue to be fascinating if the range of changes which took place during the later stages of the twentieth century continue to take place at the same rate, as all indicators suggest they will.

Just reflect on these momentous late twentieth- and early twenty-first-century events:

- The Berlin Wall was torn down in 1989 with the subsequent collapse of the Soviet Union.

- Nelson Mandela was released from prison in 1990, and apartheid in South Africa ended.

- The USA elected its first black president, Barack Obama, in 2008.

- The first mobile phone call was made in 1973. By 2008, across the world there were 4,000,394,600 subscribers (that's over 4 billion, and nearly 60 out of every 100 inhabitants!) (ITU World Telecommunication/ICT Indicators Database 2009).

- The first email programme was used in 1972, and in 2008 across the world there were 1,556,383,700 million Internet users (that's over 1.5 billion) (ITU World Telecommunication/ICT Indicators Database 2009).

With many social, technological, political and economic changes taking place around the world, it would be somewhat odd not to see this reflected in the world of education in general, and PCE in particular. The ways in which this climate of change can affect you as a teacher are however both direct and indirect.

Direct change

Direct change affects you in the immediate world of your subject, teaching and students. It can include finding out that the course you have just started getting used to after your first year is changing so significantly in the second year that you are almost starting again from scratch. The introduction of new modules, assessment tasks, verification procedures or completely new areas of the curriculum happens just months (or sometimes even weeks) before your students are due to start, and the first teaching sessions are due to take place. At the extremes the syllabus or curriculum can change *after* you have started teaching it. Piloting anything new is rare to the degree where it is probably best not to expect it. New initiatives, ideas and new approaches rain down from government, from your own institution and from the local or regional funding organisation with bewildering frequency. Each one of these is accompanied by another publication, web site or series of staff development events, all combining to produce a mountain of information to digest before real planning can take place. Whilst you are trying to absorb and manage all this direct change, your teaching is probably under the spotlight through internal teaching observations, student evaluation forms, or your participation in a teacher training course.

Indirect change

Indirect change is one step removed from the immediate world of your own specialist subject, and is often less under your control than direct change. It can often be due to new technology, whereby for example your institutional computer system may be upgraded (not an unusual occurrence), resulting sometimes in a loss of services such as email for a few hours, or even days. It's only when you haven't got something that you realise how much you rely on it, and email is one of those things. Another example may be when the senior manager running your section or department leaves, or moves into a different internal job suddenly (not unusual in PCE). The replacement may have a very different approach from the person managing you before and your situation could alter dramatically.

One thing you can expect therefore is to be in a rapidly changing world, with what at times can seem like little time to think, let alone to pause, reflect and consider the next step.

This is not to suggest that this much change is a bad thing (although to see some of the people responsible for the changes swap places with us in a reality TV programme, and see how they cope with our jobs would be interesting!). We would probably all agree that change is certainly challenging, can be unsettling, and can be at times veritably unnerving.

Change is a fact of life – get used to working with it!

When you take a more positive view of change, things can start to look somewhat different. Charles Handy (1995) argues effectively about change which 'does not have to be forced on us by crisis and calamity', and suggests change can be 'another word for learning'. He suggests that:

> Those who are always learning are those who can ride the waves of change and who see a changing world as full of opportunities not damages. They are the ones most likely to be the survivors in a time of discontinuity. They are also the enthusiasts of new ways and forms and ideas.
>
> (Handy 1995: 44)

This book tries to approach the work of a teacher in PCE very much as the 'learning approach to change'.

Thinking point: your own 'change diary'

This activity will help you to reflect on change which you have recently experienced, and use that reflection to help you manage future changes.

- Think back over your last three weeks of teaching. If you haven't started teaching yet, try to look forward to what you are expecting over the same time period.
- Create a simple 'change diary', or 'change time line', by briefly recording all the changes you have experienced. (You don't have to do this with linear text. Feel free to represent the changes in whatever way you feel suits you best.)
- Note the effects of the changes and how you feel you have coped with them.

Strategy for survival

Now you've listed all the changes, group them under two headings: first the ones where, as Handy put it, you have been 'riding the waves of change', and second those which have 'washed you into the deep end'.

- In the situations where you managed change better, try to pick out just what you did which made that happen.
- Share your own tips for managing change with other colleagues and get them to share theirs with you.
- Choose one of your more difficult 'deep end' situations and use the same approach to work out what went wrong, and how you can 'ride the waves' next time using some of your successful strategies.
- Try to put the improvements into practice as soon afterwards as possible.

How do we define post-compulsory education?

If you were trying to provide a guide to PCE, you would need to produce a new edition almost every year, as major changes take place with great regularity. Even as this book is being written, there are circumstances in place which may well redefine the sector. There is also often overlap between parts of the sector, what they provide and how the work is funded. Others have highlighted the problems with defining and describing PCE:

> The field is obviously vast, and it is becoming commonplace to talk as if PCE was about any learning that takes place outside compulsory schooling.
>
> (Armitage *et al.* 2003: 6)

> The sector has become a catch-all for the increasing areas of provision which fall outside of the compulsory schooling and higher education remit.
>
> (Fawbert 2003: 315)

> Post-compulsory education and training (PCET) in England is notable for its complexity.
>
> (Fisher and Simmons 2010: 7)

> The learning and skills sector is a very complex and diverse sector providing education for a variety of different interest groups.
>
> (Keeley-Browne 2007: 4)

Even in the quotes above you may well spot the fact that three different names for the sector are used! The most straightforward approach seems to be to ask what the different elements of the sector do or provide, and to build up the overall picture from there.

Further education

In 2008 there were 356 further education colleges in England and 430 in the UK as a whole. They ranged from specialist colleges (e.g. land-based or art and design) with a small number of students in a single location to huge, multi-site general colleges enrolling 35,000 students a year. There were also 93 sixth-form colleges, which provide the qualifications and other activities that would be part of the sixth form of a secondary school, but in a separate college which does only sixth-form work (Association of Colleges 2008). Further education works with massive numbers of people. There were over 4.5 million further education students in the UK during the academic year 2007/08, which represented a 2.5 per cent increase on 2006/07, and compares with 2.2 million in 1990/91 (The Data Service 2009).

Many FE colleges operate from more than one campus. Locations can include business parks, shopping centres, specialised vocational centres, community venues and industrial premises. From these centres colleges provide many activities and learning programmes including information technology courses, advice and information, real working environments for students to learn in the workplace, adult education, skills for life support and much more. Contracts and courses with employers in their local area, involvement in projects, initiatives, research and development, and community activity will all also feature in the portfolio of most FE colleges. Some still offer adult education courses in their local community, and many have moved into e-learning through some kind of online presence. As you can see from this description, further education is not some kind of compact, homogeneous operation, which works in the same way in every location. Even within the same college the day-to-day experience of teachers and their students can vary considerably.

Community learning and development

This part of PCE is developing and changing on an ongoing basis, and indeed in many ways goes beyond what would have previously been considered as part of the education sector. We are including it in our search for a definition of PCE, however, as it focusses on developing and improving communities for and by the people living in those communities. That is a crucial part of education. Community learning and development (CLD) has been defined as:

> a way of working with and supporting communities. We see community learning and development as central to – 'social capital' – a way of working with communities to increase the skills, confidence, networks and resources they need to tackle problems and grasp opportunities.

(Scottish Executive 2004: vii)

Lifelong Learning UK (2009) lists seven strands of CLD: community-based adult learning; community development; community education; development education; family learning; working with parents; and youth work. We would agree that not all those strands are clearly part of PCE, but the figures of those involved in CLD are significant. Approximate numbers of staff working in CLD are:

- 167,924 staff in England;
- 3,907 staff in Northern Ireland;
- 10,935 staff in Scotland;
- 4,123 staff in Wales.

There are approximately 50,000 CLD organisations, whose funding comes from a variety of sources (LLUK 2009).

Participation rates in adult learning vary across the UK, and a recent survey of participation in adult learning found that 18 per cent of adults were undertaking some sort of learning, in comparison with 23 per cent in 2002. It also found that people engaged in learning were far more likely to be from higher socio-economic groups and younger (Tuckett and Aldridge 2009). There were, however, 1.9 million adults over 19 enrolled on provision funded by the Learning and Skills Council in 2007/08 (The Data Service 2009).

So a teacher in CLD may well work teaching GCSEs, foreign languages, basic skills or other subjects as part of an adult education programme. They may work with community groups to help them learn research skills, information technology (IT) skills, confidence building and community development. The may be working for a non-governmental organisation (NGO) or charity to help members of communities home and abroad develop sustainable income. We are happy to include this dynamic and broad range of professionals in our definition of PCE.

Workplace learning

This area of PCE includes, as the title suggests, learning which is based in the workplace. This currently includes programmes such as apprenticeships, which have grown considerably from in the region of 270,000 participants in 2001/02 to just over 1 million participants under 19 in 2007/08. One current programme of job-related training, Train to Gain, grew to 346,200 starts in 2007/08, which was an increase of 67.8 per cent from 2006/07 (The Data Service 2009). Some of these participants will also feature in the other statistics, but this is again a sizeable area, which could include anything from a major multinational company employing thousands of staff and providing its own learning centre on site, to a 'micro business' employing under 10 people, where all training is done on the job. If you are teaching on workplace learning your experience could again be very different from a colleague teaching an 'academic' programme in a college, as you could be working in a local company's premises, a learning centre, a classroom, or out in the field.

14–19 provision

The UK education system is undergoing a major reform in 14–19 education, and this is involving a growing number of teachers in PCE. There are now significant numbers of 14- to 19-year-olds studying in FE colleges on either a full-time or a part-time basis. The statistics confirm this:

- In 2006/07 there were 83,000 14- to 16-year-olds enrolled at a college.
- Of all 16- to 18-year-olds, 737,000 chose to study in colleges (compared with 471,000 in all schools) (Association of Colleges 2008).
- Eighty-eight per cent of colleges are involved in delivering the new diplomas in England (Department of Children, Schools and Families 2008).

The rapidly growing provision includes vocational courses, often shared with schools and sixth-form colleges. The teaching could take place at a college site, in a shared development between schools and colleges, or in a separate specialised centre purpose built for 14–19 provision. Although this teaching would still technically be part of the 'post-compulsory' sector, you could actually often be working with children who are still at school. Our quest for a definition doesn't get any more straightforward, does it?

Public services training

One area which often gets forgotten when defining PCE, but within which hundreds of thousands of people each year undertake learning, is that of public services training. This includes the police, armed forces, fire and ambulance personnel. Those teaching in this part of PCE are often themselves members of those public services, but there are also many 'civilians' involved. The teaching can involve complex technical and vocational concepts and procedures, high-level professional knowledge, basic skills and learning support, and can take place in classrooms, training centres or on the front line in aircraft or public service vehicles. Without the professionals teaching in this part of PCE, public services would come to a standstill in no time.

Offender learning

Another area which is often forgotten, but which works with significant numbers of people across the UK, is that of offender learning, which can take place either in institutions where offenders are placed, or in the community after conviction. Targets for offender learning from 2004/05 give some indication of the scale of provision, and include:

- achieving 56,000 awards for basic skills and 120,000 awards in work-related skills for offenders in custody.
- achieving 32,000 starts in basic skills programmes and 8,000 qualifications in basic skills for offenders under supervision in the community.

(Offender Learning and Skills Service 2004: 10)

Clearly teaching offenders has its own significant characteristics and challenges, but this is another dimension of teaching in PCE.

A definition

The previous section makes it clear that attempting a definition of PCE is not without its challenges. We shall however go for the simplest definition we can, and which includes all just described:

If you are teaching in further education, community development learning, workplace learning, 14–19 provision, public services training or offender learning which is not delivered by school teachers, you are working in post-compulsory education!

Still not very simple, is it? That is the reality of PCE.

What and where you may be teaching

As you can see from the previous section, in a sector as diverse as PCE, teachers will tend to encounter a broader portfolio of teaching experiences across a relatively short period of time than in other sectors of education. To give you something of a feel for how it can be, here are six examples of imaginary but representative teachers to think about.

Megan

Megan works as a full-time teacher in a large city centre further education college, and coordinates hairdressing courses at Levels 1 and 2. Most of her time (75 per cent) is spent teaching groups of about 20 full-time students, some in mixed-level sessions where students are aiming for either a Level 1 or Level 2 award, and some in sessions specifically for one level alone. Megan also has six hours each week teaching a group of 14-year-old school pupils who are at the college on a part-time Introduction to Hairdressing programme. The college salon and its associated teaching rooms are her base area, and they have recently been refurbished. Megan has desk space in a shared office with three others in the hairdressing team, and sole use of a desktop computer. The rest of Megan's teaching time is split between teaching an evening class, which runs one evening a week throughout the academic year, and workplace training, visits and assessments to assess and internally verify candidates working out in the local area. Megan has 850 teaching hours per year.

Darryl

Darryl is employed as an employability development tutor on a 0.6 part-time contract, funded for two years, by the local authority community education department, and has a base in a small rural community education office. He has responsibility for pro-moting employability through education and training in literacy, language, numeracy and work-related skills to employees in a largely rural geographical area. Most of his teaching time is spent out in companies and community venues delivering 'taster courses' and basic skills workshops either in the companies' own premises or in one of the network of three 'learning centres' in the area. He also works as an online tutor for a special pilot 'setting up as self-employed' course, which has been developed as part of a national project for developing enterprise and entrepreneurship in local communities. His office is small and shared with two others (who are also often out), and hasn't been decorated for some time, but he has a state-of-the-art laptop computer and everything else needed to provide him with a 'mobile office' (paid for by the project). He regularly works evenings and weekends, and sometimes manages to take time off during the week to make up for that. His overall teaching caseload is associated with the targets set by the project, which contracts him to organise and run a certain amount of very short 'taster courses' in the workplace, and assist progression of some of those students on to other courses during the year. He averages 16 teaching hours each week.

Asif

Asif works full-time as an information technology tutor for a further education college, which is one of three colleges in a medium-sized city. His time is equally shared between working as part of a team of three staff in an 'open access' and open-plan computer lab with 60 computer workstations at the college main site, and a community learning centre some eight miles away in an area of the city recognised as being disadvantaged. This centre has 30 computers and offers a government-branded group of online learning programmes, backed up by face-to-face tutorials from various staff, including Asif. He has a desk in an open-plan office, used by some 15 other staff, and has sole use of a computer. All his teaching involves mixed-ability and mixed-age groups, with individuals from varying backgrounds, and there is a mixture of qualifications on offer, allowing students to work through different levels of study independently, and be given tutorial support as needed. Because of this Asif rarely uses whole class or even small group teaching, and his teaching load is 835 hours per year.

Leonora

Leonora works full-time as a training officer for a large primary healthcare trust. Seventy-five per cent of her teaching is based in the trust's training centre at one of its main sites, and she covers the personal skills and customer care components of training for various front-line trust staff including healthcare assistants, security and office staff. In addition she supervises nursing trainees, and teaches on a management diploma course for new trust staff at supervisor level or above, which is linked to a local university. Most of her group teaching sessions are with a group of 15–20 participants. The other 25 per cent of teaching time is spent visiting staff to carry out workplace assessment, and providing workplace-based tutorial support, and this can involve travelling to any of the trust's seven sites. Leonora has her own desk in a shared office space with four other trainers, and shared use of two computers between the four staff. She has a teaching load of some 200 training days per year.

Graham

Graham works as a self-employed trainer providing training and development for employers and employees to assist them with compliance and developing best practice in the area of health and safety. This ranges from short, intensive certification courses to enable employers and employees to meet their statutory requirements for health and safety, to certification for drivers of vehicles such as fork lift trucks, and assessment and internal verification as contracted by small employers, other businesses and the regional centre of a construction industry national training body. Graham can be teaching in a training room in the small business centre in which he has rented an office, or out in a company's training space, or out on site examining drivers for the practical part of their certification. His sessions can be one to one, with a small group or with a group of up to 24, depending on the training programme involved. Graham has a new computer he has bought himself, and has sole use of this in his rented office, which he shares with another trainer in the same field, who is his business partner. On average, Graham teaches 780 hours a year, but he does whatever pattern of work his clients need him to do. He can have one week or two with no teaching, followed by six continuous weeks of intensive training courses running from Monday to Saturday each week.

Sunita

Sunita is employed on a 0.75 part-time contract in a small further education college, where she teaches psychology. As it is a small college, she teaches on a variety of courses, ranging from, at the lowest level, GCSE psychology to a psychology component in the college's new foundation degree programme, set up in conjunction with a consortium of colleges and universities in her area. She also contributes psychology to the Access to Higher Education course and an Advanced Certificate in Vocational Education. As a result she teaches a wide range of age and ability levels, but generally in discrete groups ranging from 14 to 25 in size. The college main campus is undergoing refurbishment, and a new building is being added at present, which has put pressure on room space, resulting in Sunita teaching in 14 different rooms across her weekly timetable. Her office space has also been affected, so Sunita is combining working from a home office with 'hot desking' (i.e. using shared desk space) with eight other staff in her department. Sunita teaches 600 hours a year.

These six examples give you a real idea about just how varied and diverse the sector is. There are many other roles, responsibilities, timetables, locations and job descriptions for teachers in PCE, including those working with basic skills, those working with students with disabilities or learning difficulties, police and armed forces trainers and many more. As you can see, however, a teacher's life in the sector is generally varied, and you are unlikely to be bored!

Thinking point: what's yours like?

Using the same format as the pen pictures we have just considered, think about your own teaching situation.

- How is it similar and how is it different?
- Why do you think there is so much variety?
- Does this make you feel like part of a sector with a wide range of richness?

References

Armitage, A., Bryant, R., Dunnill, R., Hayes, D., Hudson, A., Kent, J., Lawes, S. and Renwick, M. (2003) *Teaching and Training in Post Compulsory Education*. Buckingham: Open University Press.

Association of Colleges (2008) *Further Education Colleges Key Facts Autumn 2008*. London: Association of Colleges.

Department of Children, Schools and Families (2008) *Press release, 19 March 2008*. London: DCSF.

Fawbert, F. (2003) *Teaching in Post Compulsory Education: Learning, Skills and Standards*. London: Continuum.

Fisher, R. and Simmons, R. (2010) What is the Lifelong Learning Sector? In J. Avis, R. Fisher and R. Thompson (eds), *Teaching in Lifelong Learning: A Guide to Theory and Practice*. Maidenhead: Open University Press.

Handy, C. (1995) *The Age of Unreason*. 3rd edition. London: Arrow.

ITU World Telecommunication/ICT Indicators Database (2009) [Online] ITU [available at] http://www.itu.int/ITU-D/ict/statistics/ (accessed 25 August 2009).

Keeley-Browne, L. (2007) *Training to Teach in the Learning & Skills Sector: From Threshold Award to QTLS*. Harlow: Pearson.

Lifelong Learning UK (LLUK) (2009) *Overview of Community Learning and Development* [Online] LLUK [available at] http://www.lluk.org/3163.htm (accessed 7 January 2010).

Offender Learning and Skills Service (2004) *The Offender's Learning Journey: Learning and Skills Provision for Adult Offenders in England*. London: OLASS.

Scottish Executive (2004) *Working and Learning Together to Build Stronger Communities*. Edinburgh: Scottish Executive.

The Data Service (2009) *Further Education Success Rates (2005/06 to 2007/08): National Level Breakdowns*. London: Data Service.

Tuckett, A. and Aldrige, F. (2009) *Narrowing Participation: The NIACE Survey on Adult Participation in Learning 2009*. London: NIACE.

3

Teaching and learning starting points

This chapter introduces some key ideas relating to teaching and learning, to help you understand the learning process, and how you will manage that process as a teacher to support and develop learning. A clear explanation of one of the most common theories about how people learn is then provided using the model of the *wheel of learning*. We continue with examples of how your teaching can help students get on the wheel of learning to develop new skills, understanding and personal autonomy. Teaching students now takes place in many locations which are not accurately described by the term classroom, and the chapter concludes by using the term 'learning site', as a more accurate description of the places in which we teach today.

What is learning all about?

We've got this far into the book, and have already mentioned teaching and learning many times. Now is the time to pause and provide some basic 'starting points' in terms of principles and practices, which can give you a framework to make sense of some of the theories of learning, whilst being able to relate it directly to your practice as a teacher.

Thinking point: good news and bad news

Pick out an experience of learning during your life which you remember as being positive, and another which you remember as being negative. Think carefully, and go back as far in your life as you wish.

- What was it about those experiences which made them positive or negative?
- Was it something about how you were taught, who taught you, who you were learning with or how you were treated as a person?
- What did you learn from the experiences, how did you learn it, and why do you think the learning took place?

Strategy for survival

The point of the exercise above is that learning experiences are extremely powerful influences on people's lives. Someone who did very badly in an exam when they were 11 years old can be scared of exams for the rest of their lives. The day your teacher told you that the story you wrote about your family was one of the best they had ever read still makes you feel happy years later. Always remember,

if past learning experiences are very powerful for you, they will also be for the people you are teaching. Take that into account right from the start.

The 'official version' of teaching and learning

Before we introduce our own guide to one of the theories about how people learn, let us start with the 'official version', or at least a series of questions about teaching and learning, which you should be aware of right from the start of your teaching career. Like schools, publicly funded provision and providers in PCE are inspected by the government. The *Common Inspection Framework* (CIF) is the structure used when provision in PCE is inspected. The Office for Standards in Education (OfSTED) carries out the inspections across the sector.

The CIF utilises questions to be asked of every provider of education, training and development, and the two overarching questions are as follows:

- Overall effectiveness

  How effective and efficient is the provider in meeting the needs of learners and other users, and why?
- Capacity to improve

  What is the provider's capacity to make and sustain improvements?

Overall there are 16 questions which are used when judgements about provision are being made, and they do give a powerful insight into what 'the official version' of teaching and learning is all about. They are complex, but becoming familiar with them now will help you deal with inspections better in the long run.

A. Outcomes for learners
A1. How well do learners achieve and enjoy their learning?
A2. How well do learners improve their economic and social well-being through learning and development?
A3. How safe do learners feel?
A4. Are learners able to make informed choices about their own health and well-being?
A5. How well do learners make a positive contribution to the community?

B. Quality of provision

B1. How effectively do teaching, training and assessment support learning and development?

B2. How effectively does the provision meet the needs and interests of users?

B3. How effectively does the provider use partnerships to develop its provision to meet learners' needs?

B4. How effective are the care, guidance and support learners receive in helping them to attain their learning goals?

C. Leadership and management

C1. How effectively do leaders and managers raise expectations and promote ambition throughout the organisation?

C2. How effectively do governors and supervisory bodies provide leadership, direction and challenge?

C3. How effectively does the provider promote the safeguarding of learners?

C4. How effectively does the provider actively promote equality and diversity, tackle discrimination and narrow the achievement gap?

C5. How effectively does the provider engage with users to support and promote improvement?

C6. How effectively does self-assessment improve the quality of the provision and outcomes for learners?

C7. How efficiently and effectively does the provider use its available resources to secure value for money?

(OfSTED 2009: 7–16)

Just when you thought you were here to teach maths, car maintenance, literacy, IT or history, along comes the Common Inspection Framework and makes your task about as big as it can get! It is worth pausing and thinking about the aspects of education which are included. The vision of the CIF is broad and deep, with the inclusion of some important key components such as equality and diversity, community cohesion, meeting the needs of and safeguarding learners, engaging with learners, working in partnership and caring and supporting learners. When you are in the midst of preparing for inspections and the massive associated bureaucracy, it is easy to lose sight of the principles which it appears to promote, even though we would all probably agree with them. However, as a teacher you would perhaps have expected at least some of this to be someone else's responsibility! Some of it of course will be. Just put yourself in the position of those providing large sums of funding for PCE, such as the government, or imagine if you were a student, parent or employer. Wouldn't you feel the CIF questions are ones which you are entitled to ask? Indeed as a teacher working in the system, wouldn't you want to ask them yourself? The student is undoubtedly placed at the centre of the teaching and learning process in this model and, as a teacher, your role can be seen to be the key contribution to 'meeting the needs' of those students.

Strategy for survival: ask those questions!

As the book progresses, more help with matters related to inspection is featured, but at this stage there are three key points to hold in your head:

- Get to know the systems, processes and procedures your organisation has put in place to prepare for inspection.

- Ask the CIF questions in relation to your teaching and that of your team, and the ways teaching and learning is managed and supported in your organisation. In addition to answering the questions, make sure you have evidence to support them.

- If you keep yourself organised and keep your admin up to date you will probably find inspection a lot less stressful.

The wheel of learning

Charles Handy, who has a useful knack of making the complex accessible, recounts an experience of being taught which goes something like this. You go into a room with a number of other people and sit down. The teacher spends most of the lesson talking to or at the class of students, who are expected to sit and listen, make notes, and only ask questions if they don't mind standing out from the crowd, or are very confident. Later on in the year, you are asked questions about the content in an examination or test. If you manage to repeat what the teacher was saying, it should mean you have learnt it. We will have all had experiences like this, and indeed we may well have even learnt from them. Handy suggests however that learning is about more than that, and we agree wholeheartedly with that idea. David Kolb (1984) described learning as something which builds and grows, as we accumulate experiences in our life, reflect on them, and adapt our behaviour as we learn new things. He explained this through the use of a *Learning Cycle*, which has four stages, and we have adapted this into our own wheel of learning (Figure 3.1). The four stages are *experience, reflection, working out* and *experimenting*. Kolb argues you need all the four stages to take place, but they need not always happen in the same order. They can happen very quickly, or can take a great deal of time, and they do at times interweave and overlap.

- Experience – This first stage on the wheel is having an experience, which may be new, or may be one you have had before.

- Reflection – The second stage is when you reflect on the experience and review which parts of the experience went well and which not so well.

- Working out – The third stage of the wheel is working out, in which you compare your reflections on this particular experience with your existing store of experiences, ideas and understandings, or your own personal theory, and you start to work out what might be new, and what adds to your previous learning. You may also recognise where the learning is not new, and may not proceed beyond this point.

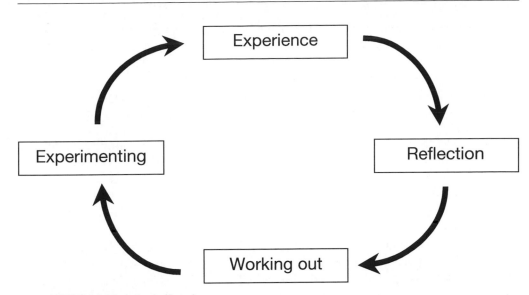

FIGURE 3.1 The wheel of learning.

- Experimenting – The fourth stage of the wheel is experimenting. Having started to build your own personal theory from the reflections and working out, this is where you try out the learning in different situations, in a deliberate way, to see if and where it works. If it works well it is added to your own collection of skills and understanding, and if not you may need to go back a stage or two in the cycle to try again.

To some degree this oversimplifies learning but, for a teacher, using the wheel as a way of helping you organise and manage learning with your students can work really well. There are many ways in which the wheel of learning could be disrupted for individuals, including personal circumstances. Think of your role as trying to keep your students (and yourself) on the wheel of learning. As Handy (1995: 48–9) says, this type of theory of learning can:

> emphasise how difficult true learning is and why the sort of deliberate change that goes with learning is so rare. This sort of learning, the one from experience and life, is the one which matters if we are to change.

The wheel of learning in practice

We can now use two representative examples of students in PCE to explore the wheel of learning.

A 'moving on with English' student

A woman of 35 has plucked up the courage to come to your evening class because she has got a promotion at work, and is struggling with the level of English needed, which was not part of her old job. At an initial meeting, she explains she needs to be able to write letters to customers on a computer. She has a computer at home, but is not very confident with using it, and her children are on it most of the time. This student has chosen to get on the wheel of learning herself by identifying joining your class as an *experience* which could help to solve her problem at work. You suggest she takes a look at a workbook which contains exercises on writing the right type of letters, and works through them with your help on one of the centre's computers. A web site with worked examples and interactive exercises about planning and writing letters is also available. A free online course in 'writing skills for work' can be signed up for later if needed. You provide a menu of various learning experiences, but how far the student goes with them is essentially her choice. She chooses to work through some of the exercises and tries the web site out, with you providing support. This experience takes two or three sessions, with her regularly talking to you about how it is going, and this shows her moving on to the second stage of the wheel, that of *reflection*. At the end of the third session you agree to chat for a tutorial, and this provides an excellent opportunity for the student to talk through her *reflections* so far. She feels she has grown in confidence but needs to check whether she has improved enough to cope with what is needed at work. This shows she has moved on to the *working out* stage of the wheel, and is starting to build her own *personal theory* as the new experiences and reflections combine. She feels she has now learnt what is needed, but needs to move on to the final stage of the wheel, which is *experimenting* with the learning in practical situations. After the tutorial she decides the best way forward will be to enrol on the 'writing skills for work' online course. Over the next few weeks she continues to come to the evening class, where you work with her on various tasks and exercises to improve her writing skills, and she completes and passes the writing skills class. Visibly growing in confidence, she chooses to join the next level of computer class, and to register for a Level 2 literacy qualification. This student has made her own use of the wheel of learning, and a number of real changes have taken place, which have gone beyond the possibilities raised from the initial problem with learning. She has not only successfully moved through all the stages, but has continued by progressing on to the first stage again, and further *experiences* which will develop further learning. Your help has been crucial in helping the student manage her experience.

A 14-year-old school excludee

You are teaching a vocational skills course with a group of school pupils who have been previously excluded from school. This includes basic training in information technology, engineering and key skills. One student is particularly disruptive and challenging from the start, and does not settle down at all to work, so you take him to one side at the first opportunity for a one-to-one session. You have decided to use the wheel of learning at the *reflection* stage, because this student already has such a powerful accumulated history of non-learning. You firstly reinforce that he is breaking the ground rules which all participants agreed to before attending, then try to clarify if he understands the limited choices which are available to him, which are to either attend these classes, or be excluded from school. In doing this you are trying to encourage reflection on the situation, and the consequences of continuing to be disruptive. On being asked if he expects college to be the same as school he indicates he isn't sure what to expect, but that 'it couldn't be worse'. The pause for reflection has helped him to use the *working out* stage of the wheel, where, despite the fact that his own *personal theory* suggests this will not work, he recognises that trying out the college course is the choice to make. You negotiate that the *experimenting* stage will involve continuing with the training sessions, and agreeing to meet a second-year student who had settling-in problems the year before. In this case the *experience* stage is used last to test out the learning from the other stages. Over the next two days he works reasonably well, attends the meeting with the second-year student, and selects what appear to be appropriate option choices. You encourage further use of reflection, working out and experimenting, by working directly with the student and using positive feedback and support. The challenge of maintaining self-discipline proves too much, however, and he is suspended from the course for three days, after verbally abusing another student and one of the other teachers. In this case the student effectively 'fell off' the wheel of learning during his experience, because his own personal theory and the resulting behaviour were so strongly established. The management of the wheel of learning was sound and it gave the student a real opportunity to take responsibility for his own learning. With a repetition of the same approach, using smaller steps at a time, even this student could make progress.

Thinking point: journeys on the wheel of learning

Think again about the positive and negative learning experiences from earlier in the chapter, and consider them as journeys on the wheel of learning. Where did you start on the wheel, and what made the process through the stages successful or unsuccessful? What would have to change in order to turn the negative experience into a successful one?

Strategy for survival

Given what we have said about learning not always working out or being positive, and the wheel of learning not always turning smoothly, the same is bound to be the case for you as a teacher and as a student. It is important to retain a sense of balance here.

You are providing opportunities for students to join the wheel of learning but they may not always wish or choose to take them. That is their choice and not your fault.

As a teacher, however, you will be presented with many opportunities to learn as an individual and a professional so:

Don't forget to stay on the wheel of learning.

The future of the classroom

The term 'classroom' still conjures up a particular image. Rows of desks are arranged in lines, there is some form of board at the front, and a desk which the teacher can sit at. The students stay in their places the whole time, apart from when it is time to leave at the end of a session, and the teacher shares their wisdom from the front. There are still many teaching rooms in PCE which would look like that if you walked in to the empty room as a visitor. They will vary in condition from the sparkling new to the old and grey, and some will have state-of-the-art technology installed, but the majority probably won't. Much excellent teaching and learning does go on in what we are describing as 'classrooms' all around the world, and this section is not intended to suggest otherwise. As a teacher in PCE, however, expecting to teach only in 'classrooms' would never prepare you for the variety of situations and locations in which you may work. One of the biggest research projects about further education, the Transforming Learning Cultures in Further Education (TLCFE) project, used the term 'sites of learning' or 'learning sites' (Bloomer and James 2001), which the authors understood as a more suitable term for a course or learning programme. This in many ways describes more accurately the locations where you may teach in such a diverse sector. A 'learning site' for our purposes is 'a location in which teaching and learning takes place'. This may or may not be a classroom. Some teachers indeed spend part of their day (or evening, or weekend) teaching anywhere in the world, without moving from their computer, through the medium of technology. This phenomenon is known as 'classrooms without walls' (McLuhan 1964).

It is the case that many teachers will still spend most, or all, of their time teaching in the same rooms, in the same building, for all of the time they teach, and there is no suggestion this is a bad thing. For some teachers today, though, the classroom as described at the start of this section is a thing of the past, and in future describing a generic classroom is likely to become even more difficult.

Thinking point: your learning sites

To help you move away from the idea that all teaching takes place in a classroom, think of, or write down, the 'learning sites' or different locations in which you normally teach over a period of two weeks.

- How many of them actually are what you would call 'classrooms'?
- What are the advantages and disadvantages of working in the different types of learning site?
- What kind of an atmosphere for learning can you help to create?

List as many of the other learning sites in which teaching takes place across your organisation.

- How many of them do you think you would be able to adapt to working in?

Some of the answers you may have come up with include:

- a practical teaching area such as a motor vehicle workshop, hair salon, kitchen, laboratory, studio, shop, art room, performance space;
- a lecture theatre;
- a gymnasium or sports hall;
- outdoor sites such as gardens, grounds, sports venues;
- workplaces such as hospitals, factories, small businesses, offices, shops;
- specialised IT facilities such as community learning centres, computer suites, open access areas, learning resource centres.

Strategy for survival: making the most of learning sites

When you look at this list, you can see that many 'classrooms' are already 'without walls' in the conventional sense, but they are all what we have called learning sites. Whatever range of learning sites your teaching takes you to, you need to make the most of them for the benefit of your students. Here are some tips which can help:

- Check out the spaces you will be teaching in before you use them.
- Find out about the facilities, resources and equipment which are available for you to use, and make sure you can use them.
- Check existing risk assessments of the space, or carry out your own.

Just remember:

it is just as possible for high-quality learning to take place in a poor-quality learning site as it is for poor-quality learning to take place in a high-quality learning site.

References

Bloomer, M. and James, D. (2001) *Educational Research in Educational Practice*. Paper presented at the Regional Conference of the South West of England Learning and Skills Research Network, 3 July 2001, Dartington Hall, Totnes.

Handy, C. (1995) *The Age of Unreason*. 3rd edition. London: Arrow.

Kolb, D. A. (1984) *Experiential Learning*. Englewood Cliffs, NJ: Prentice Hall.

McLuhan, M. (1964) *Understanding Media: The Extensions of Man*. New York: McGraw-Hill.

Office for Standards in Education (2009) *The Common Inspection Framework for Further Education and Skills*. London: OfSTED.

Don't panic

4

Meeting the initial challenges

This substantial chapter offers practical guidance on how to take a 'don't panic' approach to the early stages of a new teaching post, and provides a 'survival kit' under the title of 'Get Inducted'. This includes key strategies for settling in and finding out the things you need to know (and probably a few you'd rather not!) about your role, your job and your organisation. Understanding and developing student motivation follows as the next topic, including 'what every teacher should know about motivation'. The area which is always crucial for new teachers, planning, is introduced, with some simple planning approaches, and the chapter closes by introducing the idea of the teacher as an 'actively critical' professional. By the end of the chapter you will be at least a little less submerged in the deep end.

Get inducted

When you arrive at any new job, especially if it is your first, it naturally takes a while to settle in and to get to know how things work. Meeting and getting on with your colleagues and managers is all part of your own education about where you fit in to the scheme of things. What would be ideal is a less pressured period of time right at the start to meet the right people, reflect, prepare your teaching and generally get organised. Something like a pleasant journey on your own wheel of learning. Such a structured settling in and induction phase would indeed be a great help. You will get a well-structured and supportive induction from the best employers, which will really help you meet those initial challenges.

Often, though, you will start your work in PCE 'in at the deep end'.

Post-compulsory education is a sector which moves at a very fast pace, where the curriculum can change from term to term, let alone year to year. With a diverse and often challenging student group, and at times a bewildering array of bureaucracy to burden your desk (if you have one), your teaching situation often feels very pressured. The quantity of teaching each member of staff has on their timetable also tends to be high right from the very start of any new job, and you would be very unlikely at present to get much, if any, remission as a new or inexperienced teacher. For many people starting their teaching in PCE, 'induction' is more likely to be you starting work on one day and teaching to your full timetable with little official support or guidance on that same day. Words such as 'up the creek' and 'without a paddle' spring to mind, and can often be heard when new teachers join teacher training courses. There are some signs this may be changing but, until a proper induction becomes a legal requirement, change will be slow. If you add together the key pressures mentioned in this section, your first period as a teacher may feel more like being trapped on a large roller coaster rather than being on the 'wheel of learning'! A significant number of people do, however, like riding roller coasters, and there can certainly be some similarities in the raw energy created as you loop the loop. The positive energy from a good early teaching session in a new job is not that different from the adrenaline rush of a white knuckle ride. There are steps you can take to make the ride as a teacher smoother and less of a shock, and to make that settling in phase more effective and less hectic.

First, in the immortal words written on the front of Douglas Adams's famous *Hitchhiker's Guide to the Galaxy* (1979):

Don't Panic.

Second, adopt what we shall call the 'Get Inducted' approach.

Induction and standards

In your first three terms as a teacher, you can expect a tailored programme of training and support designed to equip you for the classroom and lay the foundations for your future development.

(Training and Development Agency 2009)

This sounds really good, doesn't it?

You may or may not be aware of the agency which has responsibility for teacher training in schools, but it is called the Training and Development Agency (TDA). The quote above unfortunately relates not to teachers in PCE, but to those in schools. The standards from TDA which teachers need to meet in their first year relate to areas such as working professionally and sharing practice; using professional development to improve your effectiveness as a teacher; effective planning; managing student behaviour; and recognising and working with students with particular needs. All of these are of course also relevant to teachers in PCE. There have been some moves towards improving induction for new teachers in PCE, and research has shown that the new Preparing to Teach in the Lifelong Learning Sector qualification has become a framework around which more new teachers are inducted than was previously the case (WMCETT 2008). With many 'trainee teachers' already employed when they start their training, but not yet qualified as teachers, induction couldn't work in the same way as it does in schools. There is much to be said however for a consistent national approach to induction for teachers in PCE, and induction standards as a requirement for employers to meet would be a real help for a teacher's early career in PCE. Ever helpful, this book provides a less formal 'Get Inducted Guide', which you can consider to be the 'deep end induction standards'. We have made use of existing induction standards to inform the content, and adapted them for our purposes. Your goal should be to arrive at a point where you can genuinely feel you have 'got inducted' through a combination of training, networking with colleagues and peers, and asking your line manager for information, support and guidance which you are entitled to. If of course the official sources of induction don't give you all you need, the advice is:

seek out and make use of your own 'official' and 'unofficial' sources of help and information, as they will all be needed to help you arrive at the 'don't panic' stage.

Thinking point and strategy for survival: 'settling in' quiz

This is the longest thinking point in the book, but at this stage it needs to be. *Do not do all of this in one go*, as we want to reduce your panic, not increase it!

You probably knew a certain amount about the organisation you are working for before you started working for them, but the 'settling in' quiz below will certainly help you to get more informed. It will help you settle in, and understand your work and your organisation better. The *strategy for survival* is to make sure that, when you come up with unanswered questions, you produce your own *action plan* to follow up where you need to. You'll need to ask these questions:

- *How* and *where* can I find out?
- *Who can* give me the answer?
- *Who will* give me the answer? (They may not be one and the same.)
- *When* shall I get the answer?

PART ONE – THE 'OFFICIAL' INDUCTION

- What induction have you had, and what has been included?
- Who are the key people you have been introduced to/made aware of (senior management; head of department; mentor/s; your course team; other relevant teachers; learning support; technical support; external verifiers)

PART TWO – THE 'OFFICIAL' INFORMATION

Much information about educational establishments is now available in the public domain, on the Internet, in the press, and published in print, either as marketing material or in the form of inspection reports, league tables etc. You should be able to find this either in your library/learning resources centre/online or in local public places such as libraries. Try to find out the following about your organisation:

- How has the organisation fared in recent inspections?

- What projects/research/development activity has the organisation been involved in and where has it been documented or published?
- Where is the organisation placed in league tables?
- Do any departments or sections have reputations for excellence, or some form of special status (e.g. Centre of Vocational Excellence; involved in European Project(s); Beacon Status)?
- What image is presented by the promotional/marketing materials?

PART THREE – THE 'UNOFFICIAL' INDUCTION AND INFORMATION

Some of the crunch questions are about how your own and your students' experiences compare with the 'official version'. Think about your own experience and ask around your colleagues and your students to answer these questions.

- How has your own experience compared with the 'official versions'?
- What appears to you to be the student view of the organisation and the teaching and learning in it?
- What is the reputation of the organisation internally, and in the local community?
- What is the morale of staff like?
- Who can you go to for help and advice as 'unofficial mentors'?
- Who should you avoid going to?
- Where can you access up-to-date documents and resources for your own courses and curriculum?
- How well do the IT facilities work, and how effective is the technical support?
- What are the best training courses to go on and why?

Don't forget the action plan!

Working with your students: motivation

As has been mentioned before, the students in PCE are as diverse a group as you can teach anywhere in education, and they can be equally diverse in terms of behaviour and motivation. All through your teaching career, you will certainly need to be able to work with students who may range from highly motivated to completely apathetic. They may even be present in the same group at the same time every week, and they may even be the same person at different times! To be able to work only with motivated students would be great, but in some ways probably less rewarding, as the challenge of stimulating motivation is a positive one. You will mainly try to manage student motivation to give all students an equal chance to learn, but developing ways of motivating your students is also an effective way of reducing disruptive or challenging behaviour.

A motivated student is unlikely to be disruptive.

We consider challenging behaviour in more detail later in the book. For now we will concentrate, as we have been doing throughout this chapter, on some introductory approaches and principles around motivation.

Susan Wallace (2002) argues that young people, who are significantly increasing in number in PCE, whilst appearing to be there out of choice, are actually choosing what is potentially the 'lesser of the evils' they are facing. Everyone who joins a learning programme, whatever their age, experience and background, will at some point experience barriers and problems which will affect their basic motivation to arrive at your teaching sessions, let alone to take part enthusiastically. Don't you sometimes wake up and think 'Do I really have to get out of bed today?' The people who are your students will also have days, hours or moments like that. It's just that some have them more often than others! This is really important because:

> Student motivation and appropriate behaviour are prerequisites for teaching and learning and in order to address either of these issues, we have to know something about our students as students.
>
> (Wallace 2002: 3)

Developing student motivation

Wallace (2002) presents a range of useful principles and strategies for working with students to develop their motivation and manage their behaviour, which centre on restoring their 'sense of agency' and giving 'them (back) some degree of choice' (p. 7). The most important of these at this stage of the book is *getting to know your students*, which is mainly about communication, not about initial assessments or needs analyses, although those have their place.

If you want to understand why your students act in the way they do, you have to listen to what they have to say, observe how they behave, and talk to and with them.

This can be difficult, especially with some students and when inappropriate or challenging behaviour takes place. It is, however, crucial (and eternally interesting) for you to be a dispassionate and objective observer and listener at the same time as teaching (in as much as anyone can be fully dispassionate and objective). In simple terms, if you can develop an understanding of your students as individuals, and as a group, and can combine that with the correct approach, planning, methods and resources, you will be able to reduce barriers to learning, and maintain student motivation.

Maslow and motivation

Understanding motivation in some detail is extremely useful in that mission of knowing and understanding your students better. Abraham Maslow (1987) described motivation as a 'hierarchy of needs', which he argued is a series of ascending stages towards achieving true potential, or 'self-actualisation'. Maslow shows that a useful educational idea can remain fresh after some years, as his work still resonates well with teachers, and the concepts involved are often used successfully by them to work with their students. The stages are normally represented as a pyramid with our most basic human needs such as safety, warmth, sleep, water and air towards the base of the pyramid, and self-actualisation, or the capacity to realise our full human potential, at the top. The process of achieving our true potential at the top of the pyramid can be seriously affected if the needs at the lower levels are neglected. In its most simple form Maslow's hierarchy, when applied to teaching, suggests that, if students are cold, uncomfortable, unwell or miserable, that will be a barrier to them achieving their learning potential. Not an idea we would want to disagree with! Maslow's ideas can be seriously questioned, but as one of a number of useful ways of looking at learning, they can be genuinely helpful.

Figure 4.1 and Table 4.1 illustrate Maslow's hierarchy of needs, and its general relevance to teaching.

TABLE 4.1 Maslow's hierarchy: levels, explanation and relevance for teaching

LEVEL OF NEED	EXPLANATION	RELEVANCE FOR TEACHING
Self-actualisation	The desire to reach what you believe to be your full potential	Are the students operating with initiative, autonomy and creativity? Is there an individual and shared sense of achievement?
Esteem	Self-esteem through achievements and being acknowledged by others	Are the students developing growing confidence and autonomy? Is there a culture of peer support and recognition?
Love and belonging	The need to belong and to be valued	Do the students all feel included? Are they treated with respect by others in the group? Are you using inclusive teaching approaches?
Safety	The need for safety and security in their world, and in the world in general	Is the physical environment safe? Are the students feeling happy and secure in the environment? Do they have overall confidence in their teacher?
Physiological	Basic needs such as food and sleep	Are the students tired and hungry?

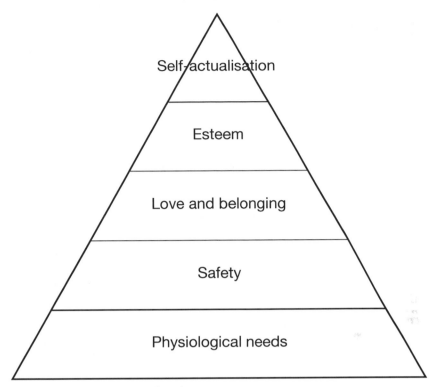

FIGURE 4.1 Maslow's hierarchy of needs.

Thinking point and strategy for survival: what all teachers should know about motivation

It is possible to produce some simple guidance for all teachers to follow which will help them maximise student motivation. Taking account of Maslow, and drawing on Claxton (1984), our guidance follows:

- If people feel threatened they are likely to stop learning.
- You need to be able to recognise what worries or threatens your students, and develop ways of making them feel safe and secure.
- Even water takes time to digest.
- Motivated students need to stay motivated.
- You can offer opportunities to learn, but you can't make everyone accept them.
- Your way of teaching always influences what students learn.
- Controlling your students may make your life easier, but helping them control themselves should be your ultimate goal.
- What works really well one day may not work at all the next day.
- What works really badly one day may work really well the next day.

Be ASSUREd with your planning

Wherever and whatever you are teaching, you always have to plan. Being able to effectively plan learning activities, sessions and programmes is one of those things we all have to do on a regular basis. Different aspects of this book address various aspects of planning, but this part of your 'Get Inducted' toolkit provides two simple models to help with your own planning. The first is the ASSURE model, which makes use of Gagne's (1985) ideas relating to the 'conditions of learning'. He argues learning is influenced by both the 'internal' conditions of the student (e.g. their experiences, attitudes, capabilities) and the 'external' conditions (e.g. the way the teaching is organised, the materials used, the location). Until relatively recent times the teacher's role has tended to be seen as the expert who imparts their special skills and understanding to fill the 'empty vessel' of the student. The notion of a teacher as someone who helps the students to learn for themselves is now however prevalent in most teacher education across the world. The ASSURE model of planning is a series of steps you can work through to focus on managing those internal and external conditions in ways which will most effectively develop learning which is more student-centred. The stages of the model are:

Analyse students

This first step is all about being aware of the needs and characteristics of your students. Much information is collected about your students as they enrol, and you will learn much about them as you teach them. You will also need to devise or use activities to collect information to help with analysis of your students. Some of the information, and how you may collect it, includes:

- *Age, ethnic group, cultural background, gender, entry level*. This is normally collected when students enrol, and should be available to you from your organisation's central administration.

- *Prior knowledge, skills and attitudes*. Some of this information may be available if students have been involved in entry assessments, or are progressing from other organisations. You can also collect it through group and individual activities, profiling, tutorials and discussion.

- *Particular circumstances or needs*. This could again be collected as students join, but can be essential to understand students and work with them effectively, and may need extra activities as above. Legally we are all required to make 'reasonable adaptations' to meet particular needs such as disability, so it is important to be able to access that information.

- *Learning styles and preferences*. Many organisations now carry out assessments of these, and can help discover, for example, whether students prefer visual approaches or hands-on approaches to learning.

Take learning styles into account in your planning but don't overemphasise their importance.

State objectives

Once you know more about your students, you can write the learning objectives for the session or course. Objectives state what the students will be able to do at the end of the session.

Select teaching methods and learning resources

The teaching methods and learning resources are the teacher's 'tools of the trade' which will help your students achieve the learning objectives. Selecting the appropriate mix of methods and resources should be guided by:

- the subject or topic involved and the methods best suited to teaching it;
- the methods which will combine to best meet a particular student's or group's needs;
- accessibility, clarity, presentation and appropriateness of the learning resources for your students in combination with the chosen methods.

Utilise methods and resources

This is when the session actually takes place, and you use the methods and resources as planned. Try out any new methods or resources before you use them, and if you are going to use technology, don't assume that everything will work. Be sure to have a plan B.

Require student participation

It is generally felt that people learn best when they are actively involved in their learning, and the wheel of learning reflects this. However you approach your teaching, it is possible to include active participation. Try using questions and answers, discussions, group work, hands-on activities, projects and other ways of getting students actively involved in the learning of the content. Use participation to listen to your students and allow them to become aware of the content. Create an atmosphere which will help them to learn as opposed to trying to 'teach' them.

Evaluate and revise

This last stage is often neglected but it is the most important one. Considering what worked well in a session and what didn't is a real challenge for us all, although I'm sure we all at least think about it. This stage is, however, about acting on those thoughts, and indeed on the thoughts of your students. Sometimes the session you thought was planned down to the final detail may not work because of one small problem. More questions than you expected and one computer in a room of 20 which didn't work, and you ended up only covering half of what was planned. On another occasion, you haven't actually had time to produce the new resources you had planned, but a really good discussion ensued in which the students got so involved that they solved the problem set in the session for themselves without the need for further resources.

We all have bad teaching sessions or days. This does not mean we are bad teachers.

If you don't spend time reflecting on your teaching, and looking for ways to improve it next time around, you will, however, miss out on being able to provide better learning.

SMART objectives

Writing learning objectives is a crucial part of teaching, and is another of those areas which new teachers can find challenging. Think of the objectives as the words that clearly describe the learning which will result from your teaching. After all, if you can't clearly describe the intended learning, how are you going to know whether your students have achieved it? SMART objectives are included here because the approach is clear and relevant, and because we have found teachers like using it. Writing objectives, as the ASSURE model makes clear, is only part of the planning picture, but it is a very important part.

SMART stands for:

- *Specific* – the students can tell what they should be able to achieve from reading the objective.

- *Measurable* – the students will be able to recognise when they have achieved the objective.

- *Achievable* – it is genuinely possible to complete the objective in the time, and with the resources available.

- *Relevant* – the objective is appropriate for the student and the situation.

- *Time bounded* – the objective has a time limit for completion.

For example:

1 By the end of the next two sessions, each team of students will devise and deliver a PowerPoint presentation on their agreed topic to the whole student group, and collect feedback on their performance by using a questionnaire.

2 By the end of this session you will follow the appropriate job sheet to remove and replace all spark plugs in the blue Mini parked in motor maintenance bay 4.

3 After working through the online life skills self-assessment, you will discuss your feelings about taking the test with two other students, and report back the results to the whole group.

If you use these tools, planning will get easier. In addition you can use them to look at syllabuses, and other programme documents, and see how they match up to the ASSURE or SMART approaches.

Thinking point: how ASSUREd or SMART are you?

- Produce a plan for about five hours of teaching using the ASSURE approach. Use the content in this section to check back on it and evaluate it when you have planned and carried out the teaching.

- Write at least six SMART objectives of your own, use them in your teaching, and review the results to see how effectively they were achieved.

- Review at least one other course document you work with to see if it is ASSUREd or SMART.

Being 'actively critical'

Much of your work early in your career as a teacher is intensely practical, and you learn much from day-to-day successes or problems. Staying afloat by concentrating on getting things done rather than spending too much time thinking about them is the natural reaction for many. We strongly argue throughout this book that:

> having a way of 'making sense of what you do' is essential for your long-term health and development as a teacher, and it will help your work and build your personal confidence.

As Killen (1989: 49) puts it:

> Having a mechanical approach to teaching may provide a teacher with immediate skill, but the skills of introspection, open-mindedness and willingness to accept responsibility for one's actions and decisions will give teachers the power to go on developing.

At this stage of the book, we are describing this approach as being 'actively critical'. It will help you to work better, feel better, survive longer and achieve more over an extended period. It is not suggested that this is a painless and problem-free process. We are presenting the teacher as someone who is constantly riding the learning wheel, gradually becoming less likely to fall off, and trying to work with others to keep the wheel turning. You will encounter problems and challenges all the time. If you wish to solve some of those problems, you need to be ready on occasions to push at some of the limits, test some of the boundaries and take occasional risks. At times you may even need to put forward ideas and suggest actions, which may not be what others want to hear. Being 'actively critical' goes beyond the technicalities of teaching, it is part of your strategy for survival. Later in the book we will take this idea further, but for now, the key characteristics we suggest you should try to develop to be 'actively critical' are:

- a determination to 'stop and think' about what you are doing on an ongoing basis;

- taking an active interest in how you and your teaching fit into the wider world;

- seeing yourself as a researcher who can improve what you do, and contribute to the broader picture;

- keeping an open mind and being ready to accept challenges;

- questioning and problematising what you do individually, with others, and in your organisation;

- engaging positively in collaboration and partnership.

So when the 'getting started' quiz throws up a person who has already taught a new course you're going to be involved in, go and see them, ask the questions, offer suggestions and make plans. When you go out into the local area and ask 20 people what your organisation does, and what they think of it, and only five have heard of it at all, go back and let your marketing department know, and ask your own students the same questions, to see what messages they are getting.

References

Adams, D. (1979) *The Hitchhiker's Guide to the Galaxy*. London: Pan Books.

Claxton. G. (1984) *Live and Learn: An Introduction to the Psychology of Growth and Change in Everyday Life*. Maidenhead: OUP.

Gagne, R. (1985) *The Conditions of Learning*. 4th edition. New York: Holt, Rinehart & Winston.

Killen, L. (1989) Reflecting on reflective teaching: a response. *Journal of Teacher Education*, 47 (1): 49–52.

Maslow, A. (1987) *Motivation and Personality*. New York: Harper and Row.

Training and Development Agency (2009) [Online] Induction [available at] http://www.tda.gov.uk/teachers/induction.aspx (accessed 18 April 2010).

Wallace, S. (2002) *Managing and Motivating Students in Further Education*. Exeter: Learning Matters.

WMCETT (2008) *QIA Professionalising the Workforce Case Studies*. Warwick: West Midlands Centre for Excellence in Teacher Training.

5

Access for all

Working with Skills for Life

This chapter introduces a major area of work for many teachers in PCE, which is skills for life. The chapter starts by briefly explaining the Skills for Life Strategy, and the scale and nature of the positive challenge this represents for PCE. A simple quiz is included to help you recognise the scale of problems associated with poor adult language, literacy and numeracy (LLN) in the UK, and how this challenges all teachers to take an active part in changing the situation. Mini case studies follow of how students' lives are disadvantaged because of difficulties associated with skills for life, and examples of how opportunities to learn can improve and transform their situations. The chapter then offers an opportunity for you to profile your own background, achievements and barriers relating to language, literacy and numeracy. Considering how this has affected your life chances and career to date will help you understand why this is so important for teachers and their students, and to relate more closely to your students' own experiences. The chapter closes with some key tips for all teachers in working with skills for life.

Skills for Life

Skills for Life is the major national government strategy to improve adult LLN skills, which was first launched in March 2001. This followed publication of what is known as the Moser Report (after the name of its chair, Sir Claus Moser) in 1999, which reviewed the state of what was then called adult basic skills, and proposed a number of key objectives aimed at improving the situation (DfES 1999). In 2009, the Skills for Life Strategy was 'refreshed' and the key intention was restated as follows:

> The Government's continued commitment to Skills for Life underpins all of our ambitions for our nation's economy and our society. That is because good literacy, language and numeracy skills underpin almost everything we do in our daily lives – at work and at home.
>
> (DIUS 2009: 3)

The strategy has four key themes.

(a) boosting demand for learning among individuals and employers

(b) ensuring there is capacity to deliver high quality provision by funding and co-ordinating the planning and delivery of provision, and diversifying the provider base

(c) raising standards by putting in place a teaching and learning infrastructure which includes a national curriculum, national tests, new quality standards and measures to professionalise the teaching workforce

(d) increasing learner achievement by removing barriers to learning and encouraging more learners to work towards a nationally recognised qualification.

(DIUS 2009: 5–6)

Considering the document is about improving skills for life, the language used is somewhat ironically cumbersome and difficult. In simple terms the strategy is intended to boost demand for skills for life training; build the capacity of organisations to provide training; train more teachers in the different aspects of teaching skills for life; and find ways of engaging more students in skills for life learning.

What does this have to do with us as teachers?

First, this is one of the biggest overarching policy drives which has ever taken place in PCE, and significant government resources (£5 billion over the first five years) have been invested in making it happen. It is not going to go away and, even if you are teaching badminton for two hours a week as part of an adult education course, it is relevant for you as a teacher. You also need to notice the emphasis is from age 16 upwards, with the majority of resources allocated to 19 plus, so most teachers in the sector will be involved in teaching this age range. As one of the key purposes of this book is to reinforce the status of teaching as a special and life-enhancing occupation, we would strongly argue that all teachers should readily join forces to help reduce the hardship and social and economic exclusion which can be caused by difficulties with LLN.

The Skills for Life agenda is not going away – embrace it with enthusiasm.

What does it mean in practical terms for most teachers who do not specialise in teaching LLN? For all teachers it is about enabling them 'to identify and to take advantage of the opportunities within their own vocational or subject area to develop the literacy, numeracy and language skills of their learners' (FENTO 2004: 3). For example, if you can help any of your students to improve their confidence with speaking, writing or maths in any way, the chances are that will have a wider positive impact on their overall confidence and achievements in learning overall.

Skills for Life has clear expectations of all teachers, and expects us all to be able to:

■ help our own students identify their own needs in relation to LLN;

■ develop approaches to supporting those needs within our teaching subject

■ achieve a minimum level of competence in our own LLN skills to underpin our teaching roles.

The scale of the challenge

When you look at some of the statistics, you will readily appreciate the scale of the problem we face in the UK. In 2006:

■ Sixteen per cent of the working-age population in England – over 5 million people – lacked functional literacy.

■ Twenty-one per cent (nearly 7 million) lacked functional numeracy.

This has an enormous effect on the UK's economy as low basic skills cost a typical business with 50 employees £165,000 a year and the UK economy as a whole a staggering £10 billion a year (Nordanglia 2008).

Thinking point: how big is the challenge?

Try to answer these questions (all asked in a quiz designed to raise awareness of Skills for Life), then take a look at the answers, which are at the end of the quiz:

1 If support were to be made available to anyone aged 16–65 who does not meet Level 2 standards (Level 2 is equivalent to GCSE grades A★ to C) in either literacy or numeracy, how many people would qualify?

    a. 26 million   b. 5 million   c. 13 million   d. 1.5 million

                                                  Source: DfES (2003).

2 What percentage of people educated to degree level or above *do not* have literacy skills at Level 2 or above?

    a. 4%   b. 18%   c. 30%   d. 20%

                                                  Source: DfES (2003).

3 What percentage of people educated to degree level or above *do not* have numeracy skills at Level 2 or above?

    a. 15%   b. 48%   c. 7%   d. 30%

                                                  Source: DfES (2003).

4 Fifty-six per cent of people with skills below Level 1 are in work. Of those, how many are working in managerial or professional occupations?

    a. 1 in 5   b. 1 in 10   c. 1 in 20   d. 1 in 3

                                                  Source: DfES (2003).

5 What percentage of children with low-level literacy skills have parents/carers with poor literacy skills?

a. 40%   b. 60%   c. 25%   d. 80%

Source: National Literacy Trust (n.d.).

6 People with Level 2 skills or above in numeracy earn an average of £24,400 per annum. Those with numeracy skills below Level 1 earn:

a. £2,200 less   b. £5,200 less   c. £8,200 less   d. £11,200 less

Source: DfES (2003).

7 Where does the UK rank among the 30 Organisation for Economic Cooperation and Development (OECD) countries in terms of skills?

a. 4th   b. 10th   c. 14th   d. 17th

Source: OECD (2006).

(Quiz based on Move On 2009.)

No cheating!

Quiz answers

1: a; 2: c; 3: b; 4: a; 5: b; 6: b; 7: d.

Strategy for survival: what can I do about it?

As with many areas of teaching, starting small can be a good way of moving forward. Clearly on your own you cannot solve the LLN problems of the nation but you can:

- Link up with the specialist advisors, tutors and guidance staff in your organisation to get advice, assistance and specialist support.

- Search the Internet for 'skills for life'. There are many good ideas and resources out there for this area of work.

- Look out for difficulties students may appear to have with literacy, language or numeracy, and how that affects their participation in your sessions.

- Add 'skills for life' as a category on your session plans. You'll be surprised how soon it becomes a regular feature.

- Don't be afraid to seek help yourself if you need to improve your own skills in this area; you are not alone.

Student case studies

Just how can the life chances of members of the community be improved though Skills for Life? The following case studies are adapted from real situations. They illustrate well how skills for life can be addressed in different and imaginative ways to make a real difference. Use the examples to develop your own practice.

Eric

Eric has spent much of his time at home in Jamaica; now he is living in England in and around musicians and studios. He has often helped operate the studio equipment, and would love to work as a sound engineer, but has real difficulties with his reading, writing and maths. A friend suggests he goes to the local college for advice, and he ends up joining an adult English and maths course. He is given work to do which relates to his interest in music technology. By the end of the first month he has shown a great deal of improvement in all areas and is surprised to find that the course is not just helpful, but also an enjoyable social and learning experience. His confidence is growing, and he has plans to take the first qualifications on the road to becoming a sound engineer.

David

David is in his late fifties and has had a variety of low-paid, unskilled jobs for most of his life after leaving school with no qualifications. He recently decided he wanted to learn how to use computers and has 'taken the plunge' by joining an introductory course at his local drop-in learning centre, which covers using computers and brushing up on maths, using online study with help from teachers in the drop-in centre. Being able to work on the course at his own pace and in his own time suits him well, and he manages to gain the final qualification in less than the normal time. He chooses to go back into factory work but is confident that he will be able to take opportunities to get promoted, and signs up for the next-level course.

Bangladeshi gardening group

A group of Bangladeshi women who regularly attended their local community centre rarely moved outside a small circle of their immediate friends and family, and few were able to speak English with confidence. They all shared an interest in growing window boxes, and the centre education worker managed to persuade them to attend a nearby city farm as a group, with an interpreter, to take part in horticulture classes. This really helped them develop their enthusiasm and skills in plant growing, but gave some enough confidence to try basic English classes, with half of the group passing an introductory certificate. At least half of them are planning to join computer classes, and the course has provided a bridge into a wider and richer outside world.

There are some key success factors contained in each of these case studies which are essential if Skills for Life is to succeed. They are that:

- The individual with skills for life challenges becomes aware that there is help and support available.
- Teachers working with adults in this area are able to make the learning accessible, personalised and enjoyable.
- Real-life improvements can be quickly be recognised by participants.
- Opportunities for progression are available and accessible.

Your own literacy, language, numeracy and ICT profile

One really good way of bringing home just what impact literacy, language and numeracy have on our lives is to look at ourselves, not just as teachers, but as individuals. Like any self-reflection, this isn't always an entirely enjoyable experience, but much of what makes you a good teacher comes from the way you make use of your life experiences in a positive way, so please treat this next activity in that spirit.

Thinking point: your individual LLN profile

- What qualifications do you have in literacy, English language or numeracy (LLN)?
- Where do you see your own strengths and weaknesses in LLN?
- How have your education, life hopes and aspirations been affected by those achievements, strengths and weaknesses to date?
- What future LLN barriers do you face in achieving your life and career goals?
- What are you planning to do to improve?

Strategy for survival: build those skills

We all recognise areas where we could improve our LLN skills. Writing reports, calculating percentages, and understanding how to use an apostrophe correctly are all regular difficulties many teachers have with their own LLN. If you have identified any major problem areas through the last thinking point, it is essential that you get support, advice and training to help. Much help is available in PCE, and as the case studies show, you can follow your own interests to develop those skills.

Don't limit your capacity; if you need assistance with LLN, ask for help.

Skills for Life teaching tips

To conclude the chapter here are some teaching tips which should help you not only with Skills for Life, but in generally using inclusive teaching approaches.

- Make sure you are always looking to improve your own skills and confidence in LLN.
- Constantly look for opportunities to include LLN within your subject teaching, starting in small ways and building up.
- Assess your students' LLN skills, previous learning and learning preferences or styles in whatever way works for you, and does not undermine their confidence.
- Look for approaches and methods of support which provide variety.
- Keep what interests and motivates your students at the centre of what you do.
- Challenge students and welcome success by accentuating the positive.
- Provide regular feedback and reinforcement opportunities, and use them to check learning.
- If students have a disability, treat them as individuals, not as conditions.
- Ask disabled students about the effects of their disability as they are the experts, and listen to what they say.

References

DfES (1999) *A Fresh Start: Improving Literacy and Numeracy*. London: Department for Education and Skills.

DfES (2003) *The Skills for Life Survey: A National Needs and Impact Survey of Literacy, Numeracy and ICT Skills*. London: DfES.

DIUS (2009) *Skills for Life: Changing Lives*. London: Department for Innovation, Universities and Skills.

FENTO (2004) *Addressing Language, Literacy and Numeracy Needs in Education and Training: Defining the Minimum Core of Teachers' Knowledge, Understanding and Personal Skill – a Guide for Initial Teacher Education Programmes*. London: Further Education National Training Organisation.

Move On (2009) *Skills for Life Awareness Quiz* [online] Move On – iroute [available at] http://www.move-on.org.uk/int_fs_scorm.asp?p=sco/m1_sflawareness/s2_awarenessquiz/body01.htm&n=SfL%20awareness%20quiz&sid=4&aid=2 (accessed 16 December 2009).

National Literacy Trust (n.d.) [online] [available at] www.literacytrust.org.uk (accessed 14 December 2009).

Nordanglia (2008) *Guide for Older Learners – Info Sheet 13*. Burton-upon-Trent: Nordanglia.

OECD (2006) *Education at a Glance 2006: OECD Indicators*. Paris: Organisation for Economic Collaboration and Development.

6

The 14–19 curriculum

This chapter first summarises the background of the 14–19 curriculum, some of the problems involved in its development, and what we may expect from it in the future. The next section presents a 'teaching 14–19 checklist', which contains key hints and tips about general strategies and specific techniques to use with 14–19. We then introduce you to the place of 'functional skills' in the 14–19 curriculum and the chapter closes with mini case studies, intended to provide examples of successful working with 14–19 students.

In transition: changes and priorities 14–19

A reasonable question to ask about PCE at present may well be 'why is there so much emphasis on 14–19?' A concern by governments, employers and education about the underachievement of young adults from some sections of society has been with us for a considerable time. Since the 1970s, when youth unemployment was very high, successive governments have tried to improve the situation with mixed results. As we are in the midst of a global recession at the end of the first decade of the twenty-first century, keeping young people in education, getting them into work and helping them to contribute to civic society remains a major concern.

Since the start of the twenty-first century reforming the 14–19 curriculum has moved to centre stage in PCE. The numbers of 14- to 19-year-olds (and in particular 14- to 16-year-olds) being taught in the sector has grown rapidly, and with that growth has come particular challenges for teachers. In 1998/99, there were some 80,000 16- and 17-year-olds studying, mainly but not only in FE colleges. As quoted earlier in this edition, in 2006/07, 737,000 16- to 18-year-olds chose to study in colleges, compared with 471,000 in all schools (AoC 2008). It has been suggested that this situation has 'left many staff feeling ill-prepared to cope with the different characteristics of these students' (Le Gallais 2004: 140).

Authoritative writers in the field (Hodgson and Spours 2002, 2007; Lumby 2007; Lumby and Wilson 2003) have all identified the key underpinning factors which make 14–19 provision such a challenge.

- Low participation and achievement

  On 2007 statistics (Organisation for Economic Co-operation and Development 2009), 71 per cent of 15- to 19-year-olds in the UK are still participating in education. The OECD average is 81.5 per cent. This places the UK at twenty-eighth out of 30 OECD countries listed. More than 5 per cent of young people reach the end of compulsory schooling with no qualifications. In addition, it has been argued that 'the relative chances of those from the middle class and those from semi-skilled and unskilled backgrounds remain much as they were decades ago' (Lumby and Wilson 2003: 534).

- The academic/vocational divide

  The 'academic' (as represented by the 'gold standard' of A levels) and 'vocational' (as represented by the troubled history of National Vocational Qualifications) components of our education system do not have parity of esteem, either from those in education or from those outside it. This is present both within PCE and in comparisons between PCE and compulsory education.

  Overall some respected writers have concluded that progress to date in this area has been limited. The following are two such examples:

  the government may have condemned the Specialised Diplomas to become a middle-track qualification for a minority of 14–19-years-olds, situated between the majority academic pathway and the sparsely populated apprenticeship route.

  (Hodgson and Spours 2007: 657)

  Reform of 14–19 education in England lurches on uncertainly.

  (Lumby 2007: 1)

  There is one key factor, however, which must be borne in mind throughout any discussions about working with 14- to 19-year-olds. By and large the young people who experience PCE do enjoy the experience:

  the experience of young people in further education is generally seen as very positive . . . the success is due to a pedagogy that makes use of experiential and social forms of learning in an environment which allows students to connect more fully to a future adult world.

  (Lumby 2007: 1)

What are the key 14–19 developments?

The 14–19 challenge has taxed many governments over some 50 years or more, and policy in this area will no doubt continue to change and develop over the next 50 years. The thrust of current developments includes:

- raising the minimum age at which young people leave education or training to 18;
- introducing new qualifications in the form of diplomas;

- reforming A levels and reviewing and updating GCSEs;
- creating new functional skills standards and qualifications in English, mathematics and information and communications technology (ICT);
- expanding apprenticeship opportunities;
- supporting learners below Level 2 and Level 1;
- returning responsibility for education and training of all young people to 18 years to local authorities;
- increasing the emphasis on science, technology, engineering and maths (adapted from DCSF 2009).

Thinking point: being Tomlinson

You can now put yourself in the position of Mike Tomlinson, who carried out the most comprehensive review of 14–19 education in recent times (although most of his recommendations were not taken up!), and at least pretend you have the power to influence the future of the 14–19 curriculum. As you are now old enough to be a teacher in PCE, it is safe to assume that you will have experienced 14–19 education in some shape or form as a pupil. From your own experience, and what you know of the experience of others, answer these questions:

- Have you experienced the academic/vocational divide?
- How long did you stay in education from 14–19?
- How did your 14–19 education affect your life prospects?
- What changes would you make to 14–19 education if you were in charge?

What does the future hold?

The exact direction which 14–19 education will take in the future is not clear, but we can be sure that:

14–19 work will be central to the future of PCE, so teachers need to be well prepared for it.

In as much as we can gaze into the future, likely implications for those working with the 14–19 curriculum, whether they work in schools or PCE, are:

- Information, advice and guidance will need to be well organised, clear and available to all students.
- The emphasis on flexibility and a personalised curriculum will have major implications for those teaching within such a curriculum.
- Some specialised training for teachers working with 14- to 19-year-olds will need to be available.

- Student support for individual students and groups of students will need to be comprehensive and well resourced.

- Parents and pupils may have their expectations raised by plans for a much more responsive approach to education.

- Partnerships and alliances between providers, employers and others will play a central role.

14–19: the students

One of the intentions of 14–19 reform is to bring a common experience to all 14- to 19-year-olds, irrespective of where and what they study, and their previous levels of achievement. As a recent evaluation of one of the key 14–19 initiatives has stated:

> in practice, however, pathfinders have tended to emphasise provision for the disaffected and/or disengaged and others for whom the academic route through conventional GCSEs to AS/A2s and beyond was considered less appropriate.
>
> (DfES 2004: 56)

In the short term at least, this provides extra challenges for teachers in PCE, including managing challenging behaviour, developing and maintaining motivation and raising the aspirations of such students.

If you find yourself teaching 14–19 students what are the key strategies and techniques you should use?

Strategy for survival: the teaching 14–19 checklist

- Make sure you are familiar with the legal and statutory responsibilities of being involved in teaching 14- to 16-year-olds, including safeguarding requirements.

- Liaise with others such as school staff to ensure the legal and statutory responsibilities are met.

- Establish and operate clear and effective systems for identifying 'at risk' students, monitoring attendance and taking action.

- Keep up to date with relevant background information about individual students or groups of students.

- Emphasise the differences between school and PCE which young students have been shown to enjoy (e.g. more adult and relaxed environment; less formal relationship with teachers; smaller class sizes).

- Recognise and take account of the differences between school and PCE which young students may have difficulty with (e.g. not used to greater freedom; more free time; less supervision).

- Ensure you have common and agreed rules for acceptable behaviour across all programmes and that they are consistently applied.

- Plan learning activities which take account of different learning styles and preferences and which emphasise activity and variety.

- Promote an ethos which recognises and celebrates achievement.

- Get regular feedback from your students about their learning and act on it.

Remember – younger students are human beings too!

Functional skills in 14–19

'Skills for life' is the most used term relating to approaches to supporting adults in developing and improving their own language, literacy and numeracy skills. 'Functional skills' is the equivalent area for 14–19. One main difference is that ICT is already a formal component in functional skills, whereas this has been proposed for some time with Skills for Life, but has not yet quite come to fruition. A 2008 guide to 14–19 diplomas describes functional skills as follows:

Functional skills are practical skills in English, mathematics, and information and communication technology (ICT) that allow learners to work confidently, effectively and independently in life . . . learners of whatever age who possess these skills can:

- participate and progress in education, training and employment

- develop and secure a broader range of aptitudes, attitudes and behaviours to make a positive contribution to the communities in which they live and work.

Functional skills are a key to success: they open doors to learning, life and work. They are a platform on which to build employability skills and the gateway to future well-being and prosperity. We all need them – they make a difference to our lives.

(LSIS 2008: 11)

Statements such as this will probably inspire and scare teachers working with functional skills in equal measure!

Developing potential: 14–19 in action

This section now takes a look at some relevant and simple examples of 14–19 in action. These mini case studies are all adapted from real situations, and provide a representative selection of imaginative and effective work within the 14–19 area.

Land-based college

A land-based further education college has a range of practical facilities and training opportunities including a working farm, stables, a lake and a climbing wall. The college felt these would be of interest to 14- to 16-year-olds in local schools. Over two years a successful programme of vocational qualifications has been developed, which attracts over 120 pupils from several local schools. The critical success factors have been:

- developing and improving information and guidance about the provision, including 'taster' sessions and interviews with college staff;
- timetabling the activities into one day of attendance per week;
- using teaching staff who volunteered, and providing them with training;
- building the confidence and self-esteem of participants through relevant practical activity, and providing them with access to the wider facilities and services of the college;
- effective communication between the college and the schools.

Imaginative work-related learning collaborations

A local authority, an employers' organisation, a further education college and a regional tourist board all wanted to develop learning projects and materials for young students. The area of the country relied heavily on tourism, so an extended assignment called 'a day to remember', which was linked to the GCSE in Leisure and Tourism, was created. The assignment involved:

- visits by students to a range of local attractions, including meetings and interviews with staff working at various levels from management to the 'shop floor';
- reviewing the attractions using a set of criteria devised by the students, and awarding them star ratings;
- developing a promotional campaign using the slogan 'a day to remember' including a leaflet and web site designed by students;
- launching the campaign to other students in their organisations, and evaluating the results.

The critical success factors of this example were:

- effective partnership working across a diverse range of organisations, aligned to a common goal;
- making full use of learning technology to enliven activity and enhance presentation of student work;
- providing significant autonomy for students undertaking the activity;
- rooting the work in real vocational situations.

The 'learning warehouse' approach

This is based on a successful project of the same name. A group of schools, colleges and universities pooled resources to set up a specialist, community-based learning facility, which could offer a range of learning opportunities in up-to-date premises with a range of technology and support services. The building is also used for business meetings and conferences, and has a café, largely staffed by 14–19 students. The environment is adult and upbeat, and a range of subject-specific computer-based learning materials are constantly available in a staffed technology resource centre. The centre is used by over 1,000 14- to 19-year-old students each year. Careers advisors have a base in the centre, which is regularly staffed.

Critical success factors of this example are:

- a varied group of organisations and authorities working together to finance, develop and support the centre;

- learning programmes and activities which enable participants to progress and achieve at their own rate;

- a unique atmosphere which is different from the normal environment the students are used to;

- advice and guidance available on site;

- other activities for adults taking place at the centre.

References

AoC (2008) *Further Education Key Facts*. London: Association of Colleges.

DCSF (2009) *Policy Objectives and Strategy* [Online] 14–19 Reform [available at] http://www.dcsf.gov.uk/14–19/index.cfm?go=site.home&sid=42 (accessed 18 December 2009).

DfES (2004) *14–19 Pathfinders: An Evaluation of the First Year*. London: DfES.

Hodgson, A. and Spours, K. (2002) Curriculum Learning and Qualifications 14–19. In *14–19 Education: Papers Arising from a Seminar Series Held at the Nuffield Foundation, December 2001–January 2002*. London: Nuffield Foundation.

Hodgson, A. and Spours, K. (2007) Specialised diplomas: transforming the 14–19 landscape in England? *Journal of Education Policy*, 22 (6): 657–673.

Le Gallais, T. (2004) The 14–19 sector: responding to change. In Coles, A. (ed.) *Teaching in Post-Compulsory Education: Policy, Practice and Values*. London: David Fulton Publishers.

LSIS (2008) *Diploma Support Programme: Preparing Practitioners. Delivering the 14–19 Education and Skills Programme: Practitioner Guide to the Diploma*. London: Learning and Skills Improvement Service.

Lumby, J. (2007) 14- to 16-year-olds in further education colleges: lessons for learning and leadership. *Journal of Vocational Education and Training*, 59 (1): 1–18.

Lumby, J. and Wilson, M. (2003) Developing 14–19 education: meeting needs and improving choice. *Journal of Education Policy*, 18 (5): 533–550.

Organisation for Economic Co-operation and Development (2009) *Education at a Glance: OECD Indicators*. Paris: OECD.

7

Information literacy

Or 'if you can't find it, use it and communicate with it yourself, how do you expect your students to?'

This chapter asks some key questions about what is often called the 'knowledge society' in which we live, and how that impacts on our students, and us as teachers. It goes on to suggest that a key feature of PCE should be the development of 'information literacy', which can help us empower our students and ourselves by using and actively managing information, rather than letting it overwhelm us. The chapter closes with a checklist and thinking point designed to help us all develop and improve our information literacy.

Information rich but content poor

We are in an age where information is everywhere. On paper it comes through our letterboxes, into our pigeon holes, off magazine racks and news stands, and we can read it while we are at work, at home or on trains, boats and planes. Electronically it comes out of our radios, TVs, DVDs, computers, mobile phones and digital cameras, arrives into our mailboxes and mobiles, and is stored on our voicemail, hard drives, memory sticks and increasingly online in our own personal storage space. At times it can feel like information is filling up the whole world, that there are traffic jams on the information superhighway, and that most mail is junk mail. Some social networking tools, such as Twitter, positively celebrate trivial information, and distribute it enthusiastically to thousands of others! Wherever you are you just can't escape it. (Just like work really!) In many ways, though, the 'information revolution' is a great thing, and at its best it can draw people and communities together. At its worst, however, it can represent something of a nightmare, creating a 'digital divide' between people and producing harassment and pressure. The situation we are increasingly finding ourselves in as a society has been described as being in

> a media society where we are information rich, but content poor.
>
> (Goethe Institute 2004: page number unknown)

Examples of this can be seen in the amount of poor information we encounter in a single day, from junk mail at home to junk email at home and work, and increasingly junk texts and phone calls. As teachers, we work with information at every stage of what we do, so we must be able to judge for ourselves what is rich and what is poor information. Even more important, however, is the need for teachers to help their students to make the same decisions, to avoid the problems of what has been described as 'information overload'.

Teaching in a knowledge society

Why do teachers need to pay any attention to this at all? If we ignore it, won't it just go away? The answer to this is certainly no, and there is a much more positive way of seeing the teacher's role as within the 'knowledge society'. What is called the 'knowledge society' is created by a combination of factors including increased globalisation, rapid developments in telecommunications and information technologies, increasing levels of automation in manufacturing processes and a growth in knowledge-intensive business. The extracts used from Hargreaves (2002) in the first edition of this book seem to resonate even more powerfully now than in 2005. He asserts that the knowledge society:

> stimulates growth and prosperity, but its relentless pursuit of profit and self-interest also strains and fragments the social order. Along with other public institutions, our schools must therefore also foster the compassion, community and cosmopolitan identity that will offset the knowledge economy's most destructive effects. The knowledge economy primarily serves the private good. The knowledge society also encompasses the public good. Our schools have to prepare young people for both of them.
>
> (Hargreaves 2002: 1)

Although this argument is presented for schools, continuing this approach to education through the process of lifelong learning and into PCE is equally important.

Education is seen as a primary force for promoting and developing the positive and connecting forces of the knowledge society, and reducing the negative forces of fragmentation and division.

Such a vision of education does present some major new challenges for teachers, and they will need to be working in areas such as:

- developing values and emotions to build character
- emphasising emotional as well as cognitive learning
- building commitments to group life
- cultivating curiosity about, and willingness to learn from other cultures

- developing responsibility to excluded groups within and beyond one's own society

(Hargreaves 2002: 4, 5)

There is a direct relationship between this approach and information literacy, as 'the key to a strong knowledge economy is not only whether people can access information. It is also about how well they can process information' (Hargreaves 2002: 3). If teachers are to help with this, the argument is clear.

Today's teachers must get a grasp of, and a grip on, the knowledge society in which their [pupils] live and will work. If teachers do not understand the knowledge society, they cannot prepare their [pupils] for it.

(Hargreaves 2002: 2)

What is information literacy?

For most things which have anything to do with education, there are a number of ways in which most issues, themes and topics can be defined. Information literacy is no different in this. The Prague declaration about information literacy resulted from a gathering of experts from 23 nations, who agreed on the following definition:

Information Literacy encompasses knowledge of one's information concerns and needs, and the ability to identify, locate, evaluate, organize and effectively create, use and communicate information to address issues or problems at hand; it is a prerequisite for participating effectively in the Information Society, and is part of the basic human right of life.

(United Nations Educational, Scientific and Cultural Organisation 2003: 1)

Information literacy should enhance learning and encourage a critical, analytical and evaluative approach to information sources which will enhance autonomy and the ability to learn. It is genuinely empowering, and we would surely want to help our students to become empowered. This is not only relevant at the upper ends of the education system. It is important also to remember that the term 'information' relates to information in general, and in all its varieties, not just the electronic forms. Many of our students are completely immersed in the information age, whatever their level of education, economic status or motivation. But at times they are so immersed that they do not think about the quality of the information involved, or whether there is any real point sending a video message to someone else in the same room. Consider these questions about your students:

- How often do they arrive at your sessions already equipped with those enhanced information skills listed at the start of this section?
- When they use the Internet, how often do they say that they have looked for information but not been able to find it?

- How often do students introduce information into their work which they have just accepted at face value, without being at all critical about its usefulness, or even its factual correctness?

Without labouring the point we would suggest that, irrespective of how convinced you are by arguments about teaching in the knowledge society, poor information literacy wastes almost as much time in the education system as anything. Improving information literacy should therefore at the very least save us all time and effort, and – who knows? – we may empower some students and teachers along the way! We cannot, however, do this unless we improve our own 'information literacy' as teachers.

What can we do to improve the situation?

First, as a teacher, encourage your organisation to prioritise and provide training and support for developing information literacy (often the province of the library, which when given the opportunity will probably do an excellent job of this, as librarians are 'information professionals'). Second, make sure you are confident in your own use of information literacy. With effective approaches to locating information, you can actually save much time, and will very rarely (especially with access to the Internet) come away with nothing. Third, what simple tips can help? If you were to search the Internet for the term 'information literacy tutorial' you would find much useful advice and information. The checklist below provides you with a ready-made tool to help you and your students improve their information literacy.

Strategy for survival: information literacy checklist

- Be clear about what you need to find out, and why you need to know it.
- Make use of what you know already.
- Ask for help if you need it.
- Keep in mind how much time you have available.
- List the places you are able to search for information.
- List ways of checking that what you get is what you need.
- Once you've collected information, separate out items which really match what you need.
- Get the key points from the information.
- Make sure you can go back to the source again easily.
- Check what you understand by talking it through with others.
- Make use of the information as you need to.

Thinking point: the tortoise and the hare

This exercise is both powerful and fun, and can be done with either your students or your colleagues, and will tell you a great deal about information literacy.

- Select two teams. One can use only the Internet (the 'Hares'), and the other (the 'Tortoises') anything else in your Learning Resources Centre (LRC, or the nearest you have to it) apart from the Internet.

- Ask both teams to find out the same information in 15 minutes (this can be on almost any theme from football to politics), which they then need to summarise back to each other.

- Make sure that the information can be found by both methods before you set the task, and try out the searches yourself first to get a good feel of what is likely to be found!

- When the groups come back together, ask them to compare the information, its value, and the means they used to collect it.

You may be surprised to discover that the tortoise quite regularly beats the hare!

References

Goethe Institute (2004) *Fly Utopia: Report on Berlin Media Art Festival*. Berlin: Goethe Institute.

Hargreaves, A. (2002) *Teaching in the Knowledge Society: Education in the Age of Insecurity*. New York: Teachers College Press.

United Nations Educational, Scientific and Cultural Organisation (2003) *The Prague Declaration: Towards an Information Literate Society*. Paris: UNESCO.

8

Positive strategies for managing change

This chapter provides an opportunity to give more attention to the nature of change in PCE, and how it can and does affect our everyday work and lives. It provides a *guide to positive change management* which should help any teacher in PCE both think about and act on the changes they encounter, move more confidently forward in the way they manage change, and work with others towards improving the future.

Being a change agent

In Part I of the book, we did take a brief look at change and some simple approaches to managing it, but, given how much change is an everyday part of PCE, we can now return to it in more detail. Michael Fullan writes powerfully about change and teachers, arguing that 'teaching at its core is a moral profession. Scratch a good teacher, and you will find a moral purpose' (Fullan 1993: 1). In many ways, this might seem something of an old-fashioned view when inspection, heavy teaching loads and initiative overload feature so prominently in the life of teachers today. We would argue that what he has to say currently has even more importance, as surely things will change for the better only if teachers are in some way actively involved in the change process. Fullan's message is that teachers can be 'change agents' and should be involved in 'making a difference' and 'bringing about improvements', which is in tune in many ways with much of the prevailing rhetoric about quality improvement and social inclusion. He continues to say that 'those skilled in change appreciate its volatile character and they explicitly seek ideas for coping with and influencing change' (Fullan 1993: 1). Post-compulsory education, despite constantly being immersed in change, does not have a great record in terms of developing its teachers as change agents or supporting them through times of change. Frank Coffield powerfully sums the degree to which teachers seem to be left out of the process of change:

> there is, however, one voice that is missing from the debate, a voice to which successive governments for over 20 years have turned a deaf ear, and yet it belongs to the only group that has the power to enhance the quality of T&L. It is the voice of tutors.

(Coffield 2009: 62)

When times are hard however, as they are at present, teachers can still help create hope and aspiration, so

> the need to be a change agent as a teacher is even more important when times are hard.

Given the levels of bureaucracy and pressures of work, simply maintaining the status quo is at times enough to keep us all very busy for all of every day. There are nevertheless ways in which we can work with change, and even drive it, so let's start here.

Thinking point: the journey to Changeville

Think of a major change which has taken place in your teaching situation in the recent past as if it has been a planned journey to a destination, which for the purposes of this activity we have called Changeville. Visualise the whole journey, from plan to arrival at the destination. Track the journey through the stages suggested below, and try to plot this visually to get an overall picture of how the different stages took place (be imaginative!). Ask these questions to help:

- Choosing the destination

  Who came up with the change and the rationale behind it?

  (Did you or others plan the journey? Why was that destination chosen? Was the cheapest means of travel chosen, or first class, and why?)

- Choosing and informing the passengers

  Who was affected by the change?

  How and by whom was the change made known to all involved?

  (Why were you in the group of passengers? When and how did you find out about the journey plans? Was there any scope for changing them at this point?)

- Check-in and departure

  As the change approached, how did arrangements for its implementation take place?

  (Was check-in quiet, calm and organised? Were there delays, overbookings or cancellations? Did you depart on time?)

- The journey

  As the change took place, what went well and what not so well, and what support was available?

  (Did you keep to time? Was there in-flight catering and movies or did you have to entertain yourself?)

- Arrival and claiming your luggage

  Overall, did the change take place effectively, and what might you alter next time around?

  (Did you arrive on schedule? Was luggage lost or damaged? Would you book with a different company next time?)

Looking at change as this kind of journey can be revealing, and can also help you plan more effectively for the next change you face.

Strategy for survival

Understanding why and how change has taken place is certainly helpful, but when you are a teacher you may not be able to choose to travel with a different company next time, so what can you do to manage change on an ongoing basis and retain some control over and influence on the situation? The next section provides a guide to positive change management based on the philosophy that

managing change positively will help you out of the deep end.

Guide to positive change management

This approach to change is based on developing personal confidence about your work, sharing and developing that with others, and using it to ensure you work more effectively with your students and your peers. It's a combination of developing individual inner strength and assertiveness to survive independently, and making use of 'strength in numbers' so that you can always find other colleagues to support you, and share the load. Remember we are trying to keep you on the wheel of learning with your students because we feel that will make you a better teacher. The process of *positive change management* involves four components.

Building your personal vision

This is all about asking yourself why you came into teaching and what difference if any you hoped to make. It may not be very clear, and once you start work as a teacher it may be even less so, as the fog of newness descends, and the demands of the job bite.

At least once a week ask yourself these three questions:

- What difference have I made this week?
- How do I want things to be next week?
- What can I do to make that happen?

This may or may not make you feel immediately better, or lead directly to you doing a better job, but it

> gives meaning to work, and it exists independently of the organisation we happen to be in. Once it gets going, it is not as private as it sounds . . . the more one takes the risk to express personal purpose, the more kindred spirits one will find.
>
> (Fullan 1993: 3)

Obviously not all the answers to the questions will always be positive ones, but you may be surprised at how often, in some way, you are making a difference. Even when the going is tough, that gives you the resolve to keep going.

Persistent questioning

This is not about being the person who always puts their head above the parapet (and usually gets shot as a result!), nor about moaning (therapeutic though that can sometimes be!), but much more a reinforcement of what we considered earlier as being 'actively critical'. It involves looking for ways of understanding what's going on and learning from it. Questioning what we are doing, and using those questions to reframe, adapt and move on, can be really helpful. This is especially true when we find ourselves in what Schon (1983) called the 'swampy lowlands', or the messy areas of our work (and the 'swampy lowlands' are everywhere in PCE!). Questioning and thinking about what you do will not always be easy, and may come up with choices and possibilities which are painful, but we would argue that being prepared to ask the questions is a choice we should all make. Here are more questions to ask at least once a week:

- What are the most positive and the most negative events which have happened in my work this week?
- Why did they happen?
- How can I repeat the positive and avoid the negative next time around?

This is all adding to your store of experiences which you can make use of in your teaching, and helps you to sort and sift what works and what doesn't.

Mastery

At a simple level, mastery is about being skilled and knowledgeable in your field; but Fullan (1993: 5) argues mastery is 'necessary for effectiveness, but it is also a means for achieving deeper understanding'. He also questions how much emphasis and value is placed on mastery in teaching, saying 'it is surprising how little attention we pay to it beyond one-shot workshops and disconnected training' (p. 6). We shall address more aspects of mastery in Part VI of the book, but add these next three questions to those you can ask yourself each week, only this time answer from the point of view of your students.

- What has got better for my students because of what I have done this week?
- What else would they still want me to improve?
- How can I develop towards mastery in that area?

As a teacher you are also an expert in a specialist subject, and in the overall business of developing and supporting learning. Mastery is an important part of that expertise.

Collaboration

Developing your personal mental strength, as well as a generally positive outlook, is important, but positive change management does not ignore the value of working with others. 'Personal strength, as long as it is open-minded . . . goes hand-in-hand with effective collaboration – in fact, without personal strength collaboration is more form than content' (Fullan 1993: 5). Think about when you successfully work with other people. When it works best, isn't it often when everyone can be themselves to some degree, whilst at the same time respecting the others in the group, and working together for common goals? Here is a final set of questions to ask yourself each week about collaboration:

- Who have I successfully collaborated with this week?
- Who have I had problems collaborating successfully with this week?
- How can we work together to reduce the gap between the two?

Try out this approach to positive change management in various ways and in various situations, and ask the questions with colleagues, or in a group. You will probably be pleasantly surprised at the common ground which develops. You may also need to say 'no' a little more often (not a word which teachers anywhere are expected to say frequently!), but be ready to explain why.

References

Coffield, F. (2009) *All You Ever Wanted to Know about Learning and Teaching but Were Too Cool to Ask*. London: Learning and Skills Network.

Fullan, M. (1993) Why teachers must become change agents. *Educational Leadership*, 50: 1–13.

Schon, D. (1983) *The Reflective Practitioner: How Professionals Think in Action*. New York: Basic Books.

9

Mentoring matters

This chapter presents definitions and key principles of mentoring and explains how and why it can be of great value to teachers, their students and their organisations. We will introduce you to examples of how mentoring should work in practice, and provide your own 'get mentored' checklist, to help you make sure that you get the support you deserve.

Why has mentoring grown in importance?

In 2003, OfSTED's survey inspection report on initial teacher training in further education found that 'many trainees, particularly those on part-time and fractional contracts, are left to fend for themselves, without adequate mentoring or wider forms of organisational support' (OfSTED 2003: 14). Since 2003, much effort and some resources have gone into improving mentoring for teachers in PCE, and many more have had access to at least good-quality support from a peer. Despite this, however, not all teachers in the sector enjoy the benefits of high-quality mentoring, and much progress still needs to be made, as is underlined by the following statements:

> The support that trainees receive from mentors was reported as being highly variable and often inadequate. The mentors themselves differed greatly in terms of experience and expertise.
>
> (Derrick 2008: 17)

> Mentors in further education colleges frequently provided trainees with good support in acquiring the specialist skills to teach their subject. Nevertheless, the quality of mentoring was still too variable and not monitored well enough to bring about overall improvement.
>
> (OfSTED 2009: 5)

What is mentoring?

Mentoring is essentially a very simple idea, which is that:

a less experienced person will benefit from time and support given by a
more experienced person.

This is hardly revolutionary, and happens to us all during our lives in our contacts
with friends, family, colleagues and others. How often have you learnt something
new from someone else more experienced, or helped someone else in the same way?
Aren't parenting and being friends at their best something like mentoring? Mentoring
of school teachers in the early stages of their careers is well established, but the picture
in PCE is much more variable. There are meaningful definitions, however, which can
help establish what we should expect from mentoring in our context, including:

Mentoring is the 'deliberate pairing of a more skilled or experienced person with
a lesser skilled or experienced one, with the agreed-upon goal of having the lesser
skilled person grow and develop.'

(Murray 2001: xiii)

Mentoring means guiding and supporting the trainee to ease through difficult
transitions; it is about smoothing the way, enabling, reassuring as well as direct-
ing, managing and instructing. It should unblock the ways to change by building
self-confidence, self-esteem and a readiness to act as well as to engage in on-going
constructive interpersonal relationships.

(Fletcher 2000: iii)

As adults and professionals we have our store of tacit knowledge and accumulated
wisdom, a result of our accumulated experiences of life and work. Encouraging us
to access that knowledge and experience, make it explicit, and use it to enhance our
professional practice, is one of the prime functions of mentoring.

(Wallace and Gravells 2005: 19)

Later in the chapter you will be introduced to our definition of mentoring.

There are tensions, contradictions and complications which can beset mentoring,
and many of these have not been fully resolved in PCE. Is it mainly for the benefit of
the new teacher or for the organisation? Is it about personal growth and development
or is it about skills and quality assurance? Just how important are the skills of the
mentor, and how can we develop them? A positive experience of mentoring can make
a real difference, just as easily as a negative experience can be disastrous.

No mentoring at all may actually be better than poor mentoring, which can
do more harm than good.

Thinking point: mentor or dementor?

If you're not sure where the title for this thinking point came from, just ask anyone you know who has children between about six and fourteen. Work on this activity with someone else. If you have not started teaching yet, make sure you pair up with someone who has.

- What do you think are the most important purposes of mentoring?
- How would you expect to be treated as a mentee, and how do you think mentoring could best be organised for you?
- What skills and training would your mentor need?
- In what ways would a mentor be able to help you develop your subject-specific teaching?
- How might all of this be recorded as part of your training and continuing professional development (CPD)?
- How does any of this compare with your actual experiences of mentoring to date?

You will probably find some of these questions are difficult to answer, as getting access to a suitable mentor could be extremely difficult if you work in a small organisation or subject team. If you happen to be the only teacher of Japanese in an organisation, is the best person to mentor you a very experienced teacher in another subject, or another less experienced foreign language teacher?

Why mentoring?

At its best, mentoring will certainly be beneficial to both the mentee and the mentor, but it could also significantly impact on your organisation in a number of positive ways. Research on mentoring in PCE has grown through the recently established Centres for Excellence in Teacher Training (CETTs). This research suggests that direct support for mentoring can enhance the teaching of individuals, build teamwork and expertise across teams and organisations, and contribute to more effective and efficient management of teaching and learning for the benefit of students. There are also indicators in the research that a systematic and continuing investment of resources in developing mentoring has not taken place to continue these improvements in PCE (Derrick 2008; Haynes 2008; Johnson 2008; Perween 2008).

A joint venture between the Association of Colleges (AoC) and the Further Education National Training Organisation (FENTO) back in 2001 did provide some useful tools for the development of more full and effective approaches to mentoring, and one wonders why it appears to have been forgotten. In this publication it suggested that mentoring should:

- link up with other quality improvement strategies;

- connect with other professional support and development opportunities;

- help to develop policies and procedures which are understood more widely, and which give staff a more shared ownership of them;

- ensure that the right people become mentors, that their roles are clear, and that they are suitably trained and supported;

- improve communication across the institution and help build a feeling of a 'community of practice'.

We would endorse this approach, and will now venture our definition of mentoring, which is:

> An essential support process which can help teachers and their organisations operate more smoothly, communicate better and value each other more, and can be a focus for developing and celebrating teaching excellence.

How mentoring can work

Mentoring has many dimensions, and will be different in many ways for each person being mentored. To help give an idea of what can be involved here are two examples of the ways in which positive mentoring can work in practice. They should suggest some approaches you may be able to try, or ask your own mentor to develop.

New teacher of health and social care in a small further education college

You're two weeks into your new job, teaching on a variety of courses in a small department, where there are two others in your immediate course team. You have been allocated a mentor who is an experienced tutor in your field but does not directly teach with you on any courses. She does work at the same site as you, and her office is in the same building. You were introduced during your induction day, and spent about 25 minutes talking about when the regular weekly mentoring sessions and observations will take place, and agreeing an action plan for the first month. You've already made informal contact with her by email and telephone three times since to ask specific questions, which have been answered either straight away or shortly afterwards. At your first formal meeting you agree to sit in on one of her sessions as an informal observer, and set a date for her to do the same with one of your sessions this week, before your first formal observation. When observing her session you can see she has a bank of regular sources and resources for her students to use when putting together assignments and presentations, and has collected them on some internal web pages, so the students have easy access, and has a filing cabinet of other resources in the classroom. Most of the sources are relevant to what you teach. She has a problem getting over a particular part of the session, and when discussing it afterwards, you suggest a way you think it could have been taught to make it work better next time. She agrees to give you access to the resource bank, but adds to your action plan that you should locate and create some more to be added to what will become a shared resource bank. You clarify what will be involved in the session she will sit in on, write up your mentee log about your first two weeks, and file it on your Record of Achievement for your teacher training course.

Work-based trainer in a hotel

You work as a supervisor in a large hotel, and spend half of each week training staff in the workplace in food hygiene, customer service and housekeeping. Most of them are working towards vocational qualifications and you are also an in-house assessor and internal verifier. You have registered for a Diploma in the Lifelong Learning Sector course to improve your qualifications, and it is a requirement of the qualification that you have workplace mentoring from a subject specialist. There is not a suitable subject mentor available in your workplace, so you have been allocated one from a regional pool, which has been organised by a consortium of local training providers and teacher training centres. Your mentor has 20 years of experience in the trade, and he works as a full-time trainer/coordinator in the training centre of a major local employer. He is available to you through:

- a schedule of fortnightly visits to your workplace;
- visits to his office by prior arrangement;
- telephone contact;
- email contact and a virtual learning environment specially designed to support this kind of regional-based mentoring.

In case he is not available you have a 'mentoring help desk number' at the consortium to contact for advice. At your first meeting you raise the issue you have regularly encountered, which is trying to assess staff who are almost always on different shift patterns from you, and your mentor agrees to:

- discuss with your line manager the amendment of shift patterns to make assessment more possible;
- encourage your employer to use the grants available locally to train more assessors.

You have a half-hour break from training so log in to the virtual learning environment and join a discussion group in your subject. Another trainer at the other end of the region has come across a complication with interpretation of performance criteria in a unit you also assess, and you join the discussion. The mentor moderating the discussion asks if anyone has any advice, and you are able to pass on information you got from an external verifier visit a short time ago, which will solve the problem. In return, the other trainer emails a new resource to the group, which is an excellent new web site.

Get mentored checklist

If you are working in a small organisation in PCE, getting a mentor allocated to you could be a major problem, as you may be the only person working in that area in your organisation. Even if you are working in a large further education college, you may still be in a team of five or six, all of whom are teaching most of the time, or possibly not in the same place at the same time very often. The 'get mentored' checklist will help you to make mentoring work for you.

The mentee

- Make sure that you have your own 'informal mentors', who are trusted and helpful colleagues, who you can and do go to for advice. If you are on a teacher training course and you are not confident about some of the academic writing, try to find a 'study mentor', who is one of your peers and can give advice and perhaps further informal support.

- If you are allocated a mentor, make sure you have someone else to go to if things don't work out in any way (the 'escape hatch').

- Protect the regular times with your mentor as appointments you never miss.

- Remember to be 'actively critical'.

- Take the initiative to look for mentor support in other places as well (e.g. professional associations; subject-based web sites and electronic forums).

The mentor

A mentoring scheme will not work without time and resources invested in it at all levels. Close links between human resources and professional development should also exist in terms of organisation, training and deployment of mentors. Criteria for mentors should include them being able to

- display a commitment to championing best practice;
- draw on a broad experience of teaching and a good understanding of how students learn;
- pass on enthusiasm and share and develop ideas and approaches;
- listen actively and respond effectively;
- support the development of effective organisational skills;
- share their understanding of organisational routines, procedures and policies;
- offer a range of perspectives and teaching and learning techniques;
- make suggestions informed by their own expertise and experience;
- help the mentee to identify practice which meets professional requirements;
- empower the mentee with the knowledge gained from their experience (adapted from AoC and FENTO 2001; Peninsula CETT 2008).

Strategy for survival

Take an active approach to getting an entitlement to mentoring which corresponds to the checklist. If you are not happy in any way, approach human resources, staff development and your senior line managers to suggest that you need to 'get mentored', and ask what they can do about it. If this is intimidating, approach someone else (such as your line manager or teacher trainer) to do it on your behalf.

References

AoC (Association of Colleges) and FENTO (Further Education National Training Organisation) (2001) *Mentoring towards Excellence*. Coventry: Learning and Skills Council.

Derrick, J. (2008) *An Investigation into the Mentoring of Trainee Teachers in the Lifelong Learning Sector in London*. London: LONCETT.

Fletcher, S. (2000) *Mentoring in Schools: A Handbook of Good Practice*. London: Kogan Page.

Haynes, G. (2008) *The Mentoring Experience of Trainees Working in Non-FE Organisations*. Plymouth: Peninsula CETT.

Johnson, D. (2008) *Small Scale Development Project at North Devon College: CETT Objective 1 Broadening Support in the Workplace, October 2007–March 2008*. Plymouth: Peninsula CETT.

Murray, M. (2001) *Beyond the Myths and Magic of Mentoring: How to Facilitate an Effective Mentoring Process*. San Francisco: Jossey Bass.

OfSTED (2003) *The Initial Training of Further Education Teachers: A Survey*. London: OfSTED.

OfSTED (2009) *The Initial Training of Further Education Teachers*. London: OfSTED.

Peninsula CETT (2008) *Handbook for Mentors with Mentees Taking an Award to Teach in the Lifelong Learning Sector*. Plymouth: Peninsula CETT.

Perween, S. (2008) *Mentoring Survey Report*. Warwick: WMCETT.

Wallace, S. and Gravells, J. (2005) *Mentoring in Further Education*. Exeter: Learning Matters.

Surviving in the classroom

10

Developing your specialist subject

This chapter firstly considers just how 'special' subjects are, what it is that makes subject specialism important, and why teachers in PCE can benefit from being 'dual professionals'. We then consider the huge array of subject-based qualifications and courses which are available in PCE, and how grouping them into 'subject families' could be a helpful way of making more sense of them all as specialist areas. We then continue by asking what being a 'specialist' can mean to you as a teacher, and the values and practical approaches which can help to place your subject at the centre of what you do. We ask you to think about the particular responsibilities that your specialist subject gives you as a teacher, and explain some of the techniques for 'putting over' your subject, or communicating it effectively to your students. The chapter closes with some thoughts about how learning technology could make developing your subject specialism and networking with others more possible in the future.

Just how 'special' is your subject?

Different views on how 'special' a particular subject is, and how that relates to general principles of teaching and learning, have been present across education for a considerable time. In a survey of teachers carried out in 2003, the results indicated that 'for secondary teachers in particular, the love of their subject ranked as the first reason for them wanting to teach and third in line of the factors behind continued motivation' (General Teaching Council 2003:2). In John Hattie's (2003) research about how teachers can make a difference, he identified 16 'critical attributes of expert teachers' (Petty 2006: 329). Many of those attributes do relate to subjects or specialisms, and the knowledge, experience and expertise involved. Overall, however, these aspects of being an expert teacher are only a part of what makes a difference, and a number of other factors are involved. In simple terms, if your teacher was the top expert in geography in the UK, but could not communicate that or make the subject interesting, it's likely their teaching would not be that effective.

The dual professional

The concept of 'dual professionalism' can be a helpful way to resolve any possible tension between being a subject specialist and being an expert in teaching and learning, and can also help you develop your own professional identity as a teacher. Jocelyn Robson (1998: 596, 597) summarised this as follows:

> In moving from one occupational area (in industry or commerce) to another (education & training) most teachers retain strong allegiances to their first occupational identity . . . this identity is what gives them credibility (as well as knowledge & skill) . . . In making the transition from one workplace to another the mature but novice teacher can experience stress of various kinds, more is involved than the simple acquisition of new skills & knowledge (in education).
> . . . the key to the culture . . . (is) the success of the first occupational socialisation process combined with . . . opportunity & incentive to develop another identity – that of the professional teacher.

Teachers who are already professionals in their specialist area (e.g. accountancy, IT, engineering, nursing) are faced with the complication, particularly early in their teaching career, of combining subject expertise with teaching expertise. This can present a number of major challenges, as it involves two types of professionalism in one, or 'dual professionalism'.

We would argue that for many teachers in PCE:

> developing as a dual professional is essential for you to be a fully effective teacher.

Subject families

If you asked about 30 school teachers at random in one secondary school what their specialist teaching subject was, a list of about 15–20 different subjects would probably be the result. If you asked a similarly random group of 30 teachers in a medium-sized further education college, or adult and community learning service, you would probably end up with a list twice as long. Some of the key reasons for this are:

- the diversity and variety of organisations operating in PCE;
- the differences which can exist within the particular types of provision offered;
- the extensive range of subjects which can be on offer within one geographical area.

In one urban area, for example, there may be six or seven further education colleges, each offering academic and vocational provision, general education and higher education. There will probably also be specialised training organisations offering work-based training in subjects such as motor vehicle maintenance and/or construction; centres aimed at supporting skills for life, language and numeracy, or computing skills; voluntary sector organisations providing training to their own workers and volunteers, and many employers providing or buying in training for their employees. Finding specialist subject titles and descriptions which cover this variety is a major challenge.

Thinking point: is everything a specialism?

This activity will help you to more fully understand the complex issue of subject specialism.

Collect prospectuses or hard copies of online course lists from three educational providers in your own geographical area. Try to include a secondary school, a further education college, and the local adult and community education service.

- Every time you see what you consider to be a different specialist subject highlight the entry.
- Once you have gone through each publication, count how many subjects you have ended up with.
- What differences are there between the number and types of subject?
- Can you group the subjects in any way that makes sense, or have the publications themselves used a meaningful grouping?
- Where does your own specialist subject fit?

If you did this with a typical medium-sized FE college prospectus, you would see over 600 separate courses on offer. Each of these will not be in an entirely different specialist subject, but you could end up with 200 different specialisms from that one prospectus! Even a small adult and community education prospectus could contain at least 40–50 subjects.

A number of 'official' groupings of subjects do already exist for various purposes. The most common in PCE would tend to be either the titles of departments in an organisation, or the 15 'sector subject areas' which OfSTED uses when inspecting PCE (OfSTED 2010). These originate from the Qualification and Curriculum Authority (The Data Service 2010). These 15 areas contain a total of some 53 sub-categories. Examples of these are 'health, public services and care', 'arts, media and publishing' and 'preparation for life and work'. Groupings of this type are clearly necessary for all kinds of purposes, but just how meaningful they are to you as a teacher is debatable. If someone at a party asks you about your job, would you say you teach (if you don't mind saying you're a teacher, of course!) basic literacy or 'preparation for life and work', or 'arts, media and publishing' or creative writing? Can we find a more helpful way of grouping subjects, which has some real meaning for teachers and which gives us all some feeling of having a 'special place' within the system? If we could identify agreed, national, meaningful subject groupings, and clarify where the smaller, more specialised teaching subjects fit into those groupings, it would be a significant step forward for PCE. The Consortium for Post Compulsory Education and

Training at the University of Huddersfield and a group of higher and further education partners have actually produced a set of 20 'specialisms' which appear to provide an example of this approach working in practice. The specialisms are used to group teacher trainees within families as part of an online community called 'OurSubject' (University of Huddersfield 2009). These are not necessarily especially meaningful in themselves, but within each specialism there is an associated list of subject titles, which most teachers would readily see as an acceptable categorising of their own subject. We would strongly endorse the use of 15–20 nationally agreed 'subject families', each with a subset of 'subject specialisms' within that family. Each teacher could be given some choice of which to be associated with, and this would form the basis of a national specialist group. Wherever a teacher worked, this specialism could follow them, but allowance could be made to update and review the situation as part of a teacher's career and professional development.

What is different about being a subject specialist?

There are certainly some aspects of teaching a particular subject which will be completely different from one subject to another. If you are teaching horticulture, for example, you are going to spend more time outside with your students than if you are teaching basic computing, and the hands-on environment will be different. If you are teaching on a Higher Education Postgraduate Diploma in healthcare management, you will need a more advanced understanding of academic research and writing in your field than if you are teaching NVQ level 1 in catering. Across these examples, however, there are also marked similarities. Horticulture and computing can sometimes overlap in areas such as garden design. Healthcare management and catering both involve people skills. Is this part of what makes the subjects special and different, or part of what makes them similar? Tricky, isn't it?

Earlier in the book we introduced the notion of 'mastery' as partly involving 'being skilled and knowledgeable in your field', but also relating to effectiveness in teaching. Depth of subject understanding is one of many dimensions of effective teaching, but we place the emphasis primarily on the 'effective teaching' rather than the subject specialism. Our definition is:

> A subject specialist is someone who is able to effectively develop, extend and teach their recognised area of specialist expertise, and who seeks to contribute to their own specialised 'community of practice'.

You could be a foremost expert in your field, but if you cannot communicate that to your students you will not be a successful teacher in PCE.

What then makes an effective subject specialist? These criteria are adapted from work produced by the University of Huddersfield (2003) and the Teacher Training Agency (2004).

A subject specialist should be able to:

■ help students develop learning in the specialist subject;

- design learning programmes in their subject which take account of current subject and curriculum developments;

- identify, adapt and use specialist teaching and learning resources;

- demonstrate an inclusive approach within their subject;

- recognise the importance of literacy, language, numeracy and learning technology within their subject;

- develop a secure and up-to-date subject base through research, professional development and evaluation of teaching activity;

- work with other teachers in their own subject;

- evaluate their own subject expertise, and update it as appropriate.

Thinking point and strategy for survival: where are you now as a subject specialist?

Using the set of criteria above, self-assess where you would consider you currently are as a subject specialist. Rate yourself between 1 and 5 (1 being low, and 5 high). Bear in mind that, if you are a new teacher, you wouldn't necessarily expect to start from a particularly high base, and even if you are a very experienced teacher you should still identify areas to improve. Decide on *three steps or actions* you can take to improve, and set yourself a specific timescale in which to achieve them. Return to the list regularly, and see how you do on an ongoing basis.

Putting it over

Whatever the subject, it is reasonable to assume that most of your students want or need to learn more about it. A number of them may already have some experience and a sense of confidence that they can learn the subject, and others may completely lack confidence in their ability to learn. Much of what a teacher does to break the subject down so that everyone can learn it involves the general skills any teacher uses. These include communicating clearly, building student confidence, effective planning, assessing appropriately and gathering student feedback through evaluation. With a specialist subject, however, comes a range of content which has its own particular nature and complexity, and sometimes it is that new complexity which is most difficult for students. One of the most important aspects of 'putting over' your specialist subject is therefore being able to present complex skills, knowledge and understanding in a way which makes it accessible and relevant for your own students. A consultation document on developing subject specialism with school teachers puts it nicely.

It is a combination of deep subject knowledge and a range of appropriate teaching and learning techniques which make for the most powerful interactions between teachers and pupils.

(DfES 2003: 2)

Whether you are trying to teach your students how to correctly screw in a screw or how to split an atom, one thing which you normally have to do is to think through how that activity, task or understanding breaks down into separate stages, steps or components. Having done that you need to then use your teaching skills to help each student put together those stages, steps or components in a way that they understand, and which meets the learning objectives of the subject. These two parts of the process are what we would describe as 'putting it over', or teaching your subject in a way that engages your students and gives them all the best chance of achieving the learning objectives. The stage of breaking down an activity into stages has been called 'task analysis' by Gagne (1985), and is a crucial part of welcoming your students to the world of your subject. If you sequence the steps in a confusing way, or find it difficult to take your students through them, important opportunities to teach your specialist subject will be lost. An excellent way of illustrating this is to analyse a task which seems so everyday as to be taken for granted, and to try to teach it to someone else.

Thinking point: cup of tea

Try to task analyse making a cup of tea, then construct a simple plan for teaching someone else to do it. (Remember the ASSURE model and SMART objectives from Chapter 4.) Imagine they have never made a cup of tea (which of course may be true!), then try to teach them how using your plan. Where and why do difficulties occur? It's not as easy as it seems, and the activity illustrates well how specialist skills and understanding need to be underpinned by effective communication and teaching strategies.

References

The Data Service (2010) *Sector Subject Areas Data Definition 2009/2010* [Online] The Data Service web site [available at] http://www.thedataservice.org.uk/datadictionary/technicaldefinitions/derivedvariables/0910/A_SSA_T1+T2.htm (accessed 1 June 2010).

DfES (2003) *Subject Specialism Consultation Document*. London: DfES.

Gagne, R. (1985). *The Conditions of Learning*. 4th edition. New York: Holt, Rinehart & Winston.

General Teaching Council (2003) *Teachers on Teaching Opinion Survey*. London: GTC.

Hattie, J. A. (2003) *Teachers Make a Difference*. Auckland: University of Auckland.

OfSTED (2010) *Handbook for the Inspection of Further Education and Skills from September 2009*. London: OfSTED.

Petty, G. (2006) *Evidence-Based Teaching: A Practical Approach*. Cheltenham: Nelson Thorne.

Robson, J. (1998) A profession in crisis. *Journal of Vocational Education*, 50 (4): 585–607.

Teacher Training Agency (2004) *Qualifying to Teach: Handbook of Guidance*. London: TTA.

University of Huddersfield (2003) *Summer School Module Handbook*. Huddersfield: PCET Consortium.

University of Huddersfield (2009) *OurSubject Moodle Specialisms*. Huddersfield: PCET Consortium.

11

Working with a diverse student body

This chapter is about developing approaches and techniques which will help your diverse range of students get the best from their learning both as individuals and as members of a group. Examples are included which illustrate how individual differences can be recognised and accommodated, and individual disadvantages reduced and overcome, with a combination of inclusive learning, personalisation and differentiation. Ways in which you can ensure that equality and diversity are both embedded in your own teaching, and valued and acted on by your students, are then explored. The theme of widening participation is included, and scenarios are provided to help you consider how new students can be attracted to your organisation, and the role you as a teacher can play in that. The chapter closes with some important advice on ways of setting targets with your students, using individual learning plans (ILPs) and the 'helping skills' which are a crucial underpinning of the teacher's role in working with diversity.

Equality, diversity and inclusive learning

In a society such as the United Kingdom great diversity exists. The best approach to equality and diversity is to see it as a rich vein of varied experiences, values, understandings and skills, which presents society with major opportunities to draw on that diversity for the benefit of all. Alongside such diversity there is also often inequality, and one of the major goals of PCE is

to work positively with the diversity of our students to reduce inequality.

If we can recognise, acknowledge and make use of diversity through our teaching this can make a major contribution to a more equal society.

Thinking point: how well do you embed equality and diversity into your teaching?

As we often do in this book, let's get you to stop and think first. There are some excellent resources available to help teachers embed equality and diversity in their teaching, and this activity is based on such an example from the Learning and Skills Improvement Service. Work through this self-audit checklist and see how well you do. Return to it regularly as you gain more teaching experience to see where you have developed and improved.

General questions

- What do you know about your students (cultural, social, ethnic, access/mobility, personal context and needs/strengths), and what do you think you should know?
- What do your students think you know about them?
- How sensitive are you/your department/course team to the needs of black or minority ethnic (BME) students and under-represented and vulnerable groups?
- Are you confident that the teaching and learning process does not reinforce stereotypes, prejudice and discrimination?
- How confident/competent are you in addressing equality and diversity issues with your students?
- What are your organisation's policies and procedures for safeguarding and dealing with complaints of harassment or discrimination?

Students and learning

- Are your students encouraged to read about/research their own and other learners' cultural, socio-economic and ethnic backgrounds?
- How do you ensure BME, under-represented and vulnerable groups can influence how their learning takes place?
- When field trips and other educational visits take place do you plan for the needs and interests of BME, under-represented and vulnerable students?
- When speakers or guest lecturers are used, do you ensure they are drawn from diverse contexts and backgrounds?
- Is equality and diversity embedded in your schemes of work, lesson plans, evaluation and self-assessment processes?
- Do students have regular opportunities to provide feedback on how inclusive (and engaging) they found the teaching and learning experience?

Resources

- Do you use a range of non-European examples and teaching and learning resources in your teaching?
- Do you ensure that all teaching and learning resources are free from stereotyping, discrimination and bias (unless this forms part of the learning)?

Adapted from QIA (2008).

Inclusive learning, personalisation and differentiation

As the last activity has no doubt confirmed, this is probably the most important, complex and demanding area of teachers' work. Overall we would argue that the key to promoting equality and diversity is to adopt *inclusive learning approaches*, and this will facilitate *personalisation* and *differentiation*. We shall come to differentiation and personalisation shortly, but let's start with inclusive learning. Our definition is:

Inclusive learning is about providing all of your students with opportunities to achieve to the best of their abilities.

In order to be able to accomplish this we need to provide an educational environment which recognises and takes real account of the fact that students have different cultural backgrounds, abilities and disabilities, learning styles, strengths and weaknesses. Alongside this we need to develop educational opportunities that meet their individual and group needs. This is partly about how we as teachers individually organise and carry out our own teaching, and partly about the overall teaching and learning context, culture and environment within which all teachers are working. By thinking about and working with our individual teaching situation, and our broader working context, it is possible to create a more flexible and inclusive teaching and learning environment for all.

Thinking point and strategy for survival: developing inclusive approaches

Being ready to support inclusive learning involves many different factors ranging from the configuration and layout of buildings and facilities to the ways in which you communicate with your students, and the handouts, web sites, books or other materials you use in teaching sessions. This activity will help you to consider some of these factors, rate how inclusive your current teaching situation really is, and plan for how you can improve it.

- Spend five minutes thinking about what any prospective student should be entitled to expect in terms of an inclusive learning experience.

- Don't just think about your own situation, think anywhere in PCE. This can work really well if you share your ideas with at least one other person.

- Generate a *top ten of inclusive learning approaches* from your discussions (don't forget there are now many legal responsibilities which underpin diversity in the UK; include them in your thinking or find out more).

- Applying this list to your own teaching situation, give a rating up to 10 out of 10 for each item on the list.

- Looking at the results, identify the main causes for concern and reasons to be cheerful *(anything under 5 would be a strong cause for concern)*.

- Decide what you can do in the next month to improve on one of the causes for concern.

- If it is an area which you cannot directly influence, find out who can, and ask them what can be done.

- Draw in others who can help, as there will be help available.

- Come back to the list in a month to see what has changed.

You must not ignore this area, as the weight of law is behind it. If you take the positive approach to equality and diversity through inclusive learning, your teaching life and the learning of your students will be much the richer for it.

Personalisation

A 2006 government consultation document defined personalisation in further education as:

> working in partnership with the learner and employer – to tailor their learning experience and pathways, according to their needs and personal objectives – in a way which delivers success.

> (DfES 2006: 7)

What you can see from this is that it is as much about the systems and ways in which educational organisations operate as it is about individual teachers. From the teacher's point of view it is mainly about putting the student at the centre of what you do, which is hardly a new idea. If you keep the following statement in the forefront of your mind, it may help:

student-centred learning is likely to help your students achieve, and should increase your own enjoyment of teaching.

Differentiation

When you actually get down to planning for the diverse needs of your student group, and when you are observed teaching by someone else, one of the things which can be seen as a good indicator of high-quality teaching is the degree to which you are really able to differentiate in your teaching. When we use the term 'differentiation' this is what we mean:

> Differentiation is about using a range of different approaches and resources to meet the needs of different groups and individuals.
>
> (Gravells 2008: 18)

This is really a simple concept. When you have a group of people learning together, there will always be differences in how they learn, what progress they make from day to day, and of course how they feel from day to day. Differentiation is about making sure, for at least some of the time you are teaching any students, that you plan and teach in ways that take account of those differences. If you teach every group in the same way with the same activities and tasks, don't be surprised if they don't make as much progress as they could. As Scales (2008) nicely puts it, 'the key to differentiation is knowing your students'.

Thinking point: planning for differentiation

- Choose one of the groups you teach.
- Think of a topic you will be teaching them at some point.
- Given what you know about the students, think of how you could plan for differentiation for that topic. (You could use a common task but offer different levels of achievement within it; you could use different tasks for different students or groups of students; you could draw in extra support for learners who need it.)
- Produce an outline lesson plan for the topic and try it out next time you get the chance.

One key thing to remember about inclusive learning, personalisation and differentiation is the following:

student-centred learning should benefit every individual in your group, but you shouldn't forget that one of the best ways to meet individual needs is through group-based learning.

Widening participation and engaging new students

According to the European Commission (2009) adult participation in lifelong learning in the UK in 2006 was 27 per cent of the 25- to 64-year-old population. Although this is high for Europe, being the third highest of 27 countries, it still means 74 per cent are not involved in lifelong learning. In an era when participation in education has been increasing for a large proportion of the time, inequalities in income and attainment have not been reduced as significantly as they may have been. Research and statistics in this area tend to show that the same groups who have consistently not engaged in learning over the last 20 years are still not doing so. Overall, despite generally reasonably healthy participation rates:

> if you are elderly or unqualified, have problems with literacy, language or numeracy, or live in a deprived area, you will be up to 50 per cent less likely to participate in learning than other members of society.

Post-compulsory education has a very good record generally for drawing in new students and working with more disadvantaged groups, but, as the statistics above show, there is much still to be done. You may well have students in your groups who are new to learning, or are making a fresh start. Taking account of that fact in your teaching is essential.

Widening participation scenarios

These scenarios are based on real projects which engaged groups and individuals who had not been participating in learning. Read the scenario, and consider what actions could be taken to engage the students concerned.

Homeless

A group of homeless adults has been selling a well-known publication in town centres, which has provided basic subsistence for the vendors, but has not moved them on from homelessness, and out of substance abuse. The voluntary organisation working with them has approached your organisation for assistance with training to help move their clients forward.

Craft workshop

A local community centre has a group of Asian women who regularly come to the centre, and who have expressed an interest in coming together to work on creative textile projects. In many cases English is not their first language, and they range in age from 35 to 75. They are not going to want to gain qualifications but would like to give a 'craft workshop' a try.

Employee engagement

You have been appointed as an 'employee engagement' worker, and your task is to meet a recruitment target of 100 new students from small and medium-sized enterprises (SMEs) in your local semi-rural area, and to concentrate on training which can enhance the language, literacy and numeracy skills of the participants. What do you do for your first two weeks?

Get engaged

There are published 'characteristics of good practice' in this field (Crawley 2002; LSDA 2002, 2003). We have drawn on these to produce *get engaged questions* about the teaching aspects of engaging new students:

- Is equality of opportunity genuinely embedded into the ethos and operation of your organisation?
- Are you aware and taking account of your statutory responsibilities?
- What entitlement to practical, financial and learning support is available?
- Are you aware of the profile of your local community, and how that is reflected in those participating in learning with your organisation?
- How flexible is the curriculum and teaching and learning you can offer?
- Do you feature diversity in your own curriculum and planning?
- Does your curriculum promote progression in clear and manageable steps?

Target setting

Now you have recruited your diverse group of students, how can you work with them to make the most of that diversity in terms of achievement? As a teacher in PCE, one thing you can be sure of is that you will come in contact with targets on a very regular basis. There will be targets relating to recruiting and keeping your students, getting them qualified and encouraging them to come back and study more. There are national targets for improving skills for life, expanding learning through electronic means, developing the teaching workforce, increasing those qualified to certain levels, and many, many, many more. As a recent report on evaluation in the voluntary and community sector has commented, however, we have to be careful not to get into the situation where it can become a case of *Hitting the Target, Missing the Point* (Crawley 2004). In other words:

> we must make sure targets assist us in our work to support equality and diversity through learning, rather than get in the way.

Providing real and meaningful challenges to stimulate and motivate our students is one of the most effective means of moving from engagement to achievement. This is where target setting can be really useful. Once we have successfully attracted new students to take up our learning opportunities we would all want to make sure they are helped to stay, progress and achieve. A helpful model of target setting in this context is described by Martinez (2001:1), who suggests that, 'without challenge, students will not be able to achieve to the best of their abilities.' This is not, however, a simple task:

> For targets to be both challenging and achievable it is important to consider the process of teaching and learning. Targets need to be negotiated and agreed with the tutor but owned by the student. This ownership has cognitive, emotional and motivating elements. Managing the relationship between challenge and achievability for

the individual student or trainee demands a high degree of skill and professional expertise on the part of the tutor.

(Martinez 2001: 1)

Here are some hints and tips for getting to grips with targets in general terms:

- Create targets which can be flexible and adaptable in line with changing circumstances. They must not end up as immovable and unhelpful.
- Make time for target setting, monitoring, review and adjustment.
- Welcome other staff's involvement in setting targets, but keep overall control where you are the lead teacher.
- Use relevant specialist tutorial or support staff as appropriate.

Starting points: SCAM

Despite the unfortunate acronym, Martinez (2001) provides a really helpful model of target setting. It is similar in a number of ways to the writing of SMART objectives introduced earlier in the book. The starting point here is that:

> targets should be *specific*, *challenging*, *achievable* and *measurable*.

Targets may be set with both individuals and groups, but remember that ownership by the student is essential.

Specific

Specific targets have to be informed and up to date, so there is a need to collect and record information to back this up. Every attempt to help your students to self-assess should be taken. If you don't know where a particular person is starting from, how can you help them set targets relating to where they could be going next? The backup information will include diagnostic assessments, prior experiences and achievements, expectations, tutorial and progress records, and general goals.

Examples of specific targets could be to:

- achieve 100 per cent attendance for the next module;
- observe the behaviour of one of your brothers or sisters for five minutes and make notes;
- write a letter to book a hotel room for two nights.

Challenging

What is challenging for one student will of course be straightforward for another, and this is where a combination of the students driving the target setting and the quality of the teacher's interaction with the student becomes central. Negotiation of a minimum starting point, and taking account of any particular course-related or student-related circumstances, needs to be incorporated.

Examples of challenging targets could be to:

- improve attendance from 60 per cent to 90 per cent for the next module;
- practice a minimum of two and a maximum of five of the required welding joints in the workshop over the next week;
- work on a group presentation in a cooperative manner ensuring equality of contribution.

Achievable

Working out what may be achievable for your group of students is something that you, the teacher, always get a feel for quite quickly. Each of your students also arrives already with their own view of just what they can and will achieve, which may change dramatically for the better or for the worse once they get started. Target setting is a way of establishing what could be described as a 'personal pathway' to achievement for each student, so making sure targets are achievable is crucial. Agreeing on the minimum expectations, but promoting the idea of exceeding that minimum wherever possible, underpins this. We would not want to push our students beyond their capabilities, but we would equally not want them to fall below what they would reasonably hope to achieve. Of the targets already provided as examples, can you identify any potential problems around how achievable they are?

Measurable

Unless the targets are measurable, it is going to be difficult to recognise whether they have been achieved or not, so this stage is about a combination of being clear and keeping good records. Two of the above examples could be made more measurable as follows:

- Provide a signed-off job sheet by next week indicating completion of a minimum of two and a maximum of five practice welding joints from the required selection.
- Provide verbal confirmation from other group members that you contributed in a cooperative and non-dominant manner.

If you still need encouragement, take heart from Martinez (2001: 5) when he says:

the best argument for implementing target setting processes is that they work. The evidence for this comes from two main types of research – large-scale international reviews of educational research on effective teaching and small-scale case studies mainly from England.

Individual learning plans

Given the degree to which this chapter has promoted and discussed student-centred and inclusive learning approaches, it would be easy to imagine the mass of processes, procedures, information and documentation which could be needed to back up the process; especially when we are rightly held to account for how well we are doing it.

For students and teachers, there is an easy answer to this in the form of individual learning plans, or ILPs. You may well be provided with a form of ILP as a means of recording student progress or getting your students to do so themselves. They will not always be easy to use but, if they are used by all, kept up to date, and personalised by the students themselves, they can be really important, straightforward and useful documents.

Thinking point: devise your own ILP

If you were designing an ILP for your own situation as a teacher, how would you:

- summarise your starting points?
- set goals and targets?
- review progress on those goals and targets?
- choose to record the results (written, video diary, blog etc.)?
- use this with your students?

Helping skills

This chapter has now addressed inclusive teaching, personalisation, differentiation, engaging new students, target setting and ILPs, all of which are areas of your teaching which require a sophisticated and advanced set of skills, many of which are to do with communicating and interacting with your students positively. The knowledge and techniques which can connect all these areas have been described as 'helping skills', with the teacher operating as a 'skilled helper'. The best-known model in this field is called the 'three-stage model of helping' and is derived from Gerard Egan's work, including the text *The Skilled Helper* (1994). Egan drew his theory from works by Carl Rogers during the 1970s and 1980s, such as *Freedom to Learn* (Rogers and Freiberg 1993). Rogers was one of a number of people who developed what has become known as the 'person-centred approach', a philosophy according to which each human being is unique in their own right, and sees their own world in their own way. The qualities of 'empathetic understanding, acceptance and sincerity' are seen as essential when human beings relate to each other, and can provide opportunities for personal growth.

Egan developed this philosophy into an approach whereby a 'skilled helper' can assist personal growth through what has become known as the 'three-stage model of helping'. These stages are:

1 *exploration* (i.e. where am I now?);

2 *new understanding* (i.e. where would I like to be?);

3 *action* (i.e. how can I get there?).

The 'helping skills' which are needed to assist others in moving through these stages are complex, but there are some basic helping skills which all teachers would benefit from developing:

- *Attending*. Show visibly that you are attending to your students as a group and individually. This is through a combination of an open and positive posture, making eye contact, and being relaxed with them.

- *Active listening*. This is paying attention to the content and the feelings being conveyed by your students, and acknowledging both.

- *Reflecting*. Mirror what your students are feeling in ways which will help them to understand the potential consequences.

- *Encouraging*. This uses ways of getting your students to think for themselves and understand their own feelings and actions.

- *Questioning*. This is being able to ask questions which clarify and help students focus on making their own choices and decisions, and recognising the consequences.

Thinking point: are you listening?

Think of a situation in which you are with a group of other people or an individual. How much do you use the 'helping skills' listed above? Are you an 'active listener'? Do you 'attend' to others? The chances are you won't say 'yes' to all of these all the time, as it demands a huge amount of concentration, and the skills concerned are subtle and difficult to acquire.

Strategy for survival

Practice those helping skills, as improving them can enhance your capacity to interact positively with your students considerably. As usual, start small. Spend one minute listening to another person, then summarise back to them what they have said, and how you read the way they felt while saying it. You'll be really surprised how much this can improve your capacity to listen actively.

Helping skills are at the centre of inclusive teaching so don't neglect them.

References

Crawley, Janice (2004) *Hitting the Target, Missing the Point*. London: Trust and Foundation News.

Crawley, Jim (2002) *Staff Checklist for Widening Participation*. Bristol: University of the West of England.

DfES (2006) *Personalising Further Education: Developing a Vision*. London: Department for Education and Skills.

Egan, G. (1994) *The Skilled Helper*. California: Brooks/Cole Pubs.

European Commission (2009) *Annexes: Standing Group on Indicators and Benchmarks*. Brussels: EC.

Gravells, A. (2008) *Preparing to Teach in the Lifelong Learning Sector*. 3rd edition. Exeter: Learning Matters.

LSDA (2002) *Equality and Diversity in Adult and Community Learning: A Guide for Managers.* London: Learning and Skills Development Agency.

LSDA (2003) *Widening Adult Participation: Ways to Extend Good Practice. A Research Report for the Learning and Skills Council.* London: Learning and Skills Development Agency.

Martinez, P. (2001) *Great Expectations: Setting Targets for Students.* London: LSDA.

QIA (2008) *Equality and Diversity Teaching and Learning Audit Proforma.* London: Quality Improvement Agency.

Rogers, C. and Freiberg, H. J. (1993) *Freedom to Learn.* 3rd edition. New York: Merrill.

Scales, P. (2008) *Teaching in the Lifelong Learning Sector.* Maidenhead: Open University Press.

12

Managing challenging behaviour

All teachers will encounter challenging behaviour during their career, and some of it will surely be from their students!

Challenging behaviour can take many forms, from a minor disagreement or excessive verbal enthusiasm in a group, to physical intimidation, and even violence in a teaching session. A book such as this cannot provide you with a full set of strategies and techniques to manage that challenging behaviour, but it can give you some worthwhile starting points. This chapter first introduces our broad definition of challenging behaviour, then a well-known approach to group dynamics, which helps understand how groups work, and through that how you can manage your own groups to reduce the chances of challenging behaviour. The chapter then moves on to consider the other types of behaviour which you may need to learn how to manage. Key techniques to use when managing challenging behaviour, linked to short case studies involving behaviour problems, follow. The chapter concludes by reinforcing the idea that behaviour management is an organisational issue as much as a teaching issue.

Defining challenging behaviour

First, what exactly do we mean by 'challenging behaviour'? It is likely that your own definition will largely depend on when and how you experience it (or even when you behave in a challenging way yourself). Aggression or violence towards you or others; not carrying out tasks or activities in teaching sessions; talking constantly; winding everyone up; disrupting the work of others; dominating a group discussion – these could all be described as challenging behaviours. Our own definition, which is intended to be useful to all readers of this book, is:

behaviour by individuals and groups which causes others problems, and which limits the potential of all concerned to learn and live their lives in as full and free a manner as possible.

Groups and group dynamics

When people come together in groups for any purpose, it is generally accepted that the behaviour of the group moves through certain stages and changes, some of which are positive and helpful, and some less so. If as a teacher you are aware of these changes, and can influence how and when they take place, you can help the group function effectively, rather than becoming dysfunctional. A widely recognised description of these stages has been produced by Tuckman (1965), which we will summarise here, with the help of an excellent explanatory paper from the Catalyst Consulting Group (1999). The four stages are called Forming, Storming, Norming and Performing. Any group may move backwards and forwards between stages, but is more likely to operate effectively in the last two than the first two. Table 12.1 explains what each stage involves, and the implications for the teacher.

Thinking point: storming or performing?

Consider one group you teach, or one you have been a member of. Using Tuckman's model, reflect on the progress (or lack of) of that group and how (or if) it moved through the different stages. How did you as an individual influence the way the group operated? What could you and the group have done differently?

Just for fun, think about your own organisation as a group of people: where is it currently in Tuckman's stages, and why?

Strategy for survival

As the person most engaged in trying to balance the group dynamic towards positive results, there are some simple guidelines you can follow:

- Be particularly attentive to the group in the early stages.
- Promote give and take and some degree of autonomy but step in when forming and storming appear to be negatively affecting individuals within the group.
- Promote peer responsibility. A self-regulating learning group can be much more effective than a teacher-regulated one.
- Expect some ups and downs, as there almost always will be.
- No group is ever exactly the same as another, so be ready for that.

Types of challenging behaviour

Minor aspects of challenging behaviour can be managed in ways which are covered in other parts of this book, so we concentrate in this section on the more extreme examples. Teachers in PCE are being faced with more cases of challenging behaviour as they work more with a diverse and challenging student group, and in particular

TABLE 12.1 Stages in the formation of a group

STAGE AND GROUP BEHAVIOURS	TEACHER ACTIVITY AT EACH STAGE
Forming	
Purpose and goals are unclear	Provide opportunities for clarification, information and advice and encourage cooperation to establish common goals
Members feel varying degrees of commitment	Find out more about the group and encourage them to share personal expectations and interests
Members are cautious, don't start things off and avoid responsibility	Clarify rules and expectations including accountability, recognition and rewards
Communication is low and a few members often dominate	Find out who has what to contribute, and consider how they may be able to do so
Members are dependent on directive leadership	
Storming	
Differences and confusion arise over goals and roles, and there are struggles over approaches, direction and control	Involve everyone in discussion and decision making
Members react towards leadership with counterproductive behaviours	Check out differences, include all ideas and opinions and raise difficult issues where necessary
They are uncertain about how to deal with issues openly	
Communication is not working effectively and decision making takes place through dominance, power plays and compromise	Help to clarify purpose and develop a common approach
Members act independently without reference to the group	Help the group make the best use of the personal resources they have
Norming	
Group gains confidence, feels a sense of momentum. 'What', 'how', 'who' and 'when' become clarified	Provide encouragement, build consensus and provide feedback through facilitating open discussion
Agreement by most on approaches, goals, communication and leadership roles emerges	Provide opportunities for others to move into leading roles
Decision making by consensus with some delegation to smaller subgroups	Encourage group to interact more with outsiders
Performing	
Members take full responsibility for tasks and relationships, and work proactively for the benefit of the group	Help the group to assess and evaluate results of activity against purpose and external requirements
Group achieves effective and satisfying results and recognises that achievement	Celebrate successes: reward and recognise individuals and group achievements
Group becomes self-organising and more independent individually but still able to operate as a group	Promote further improvement within the group

when they work with 14–19 programmes. In a study of school teachers' perceptions of pupils' challenging behaviour, the strength of feeling on this issue was emphasised:

> Results indicate that teachers are concerned about challenging behaviour and find it stressful. Whilst considering themselves to be effective in dealing with it, a proportion report feeling frustrated by it, angry, upset and/or at a loss.
>
> (Male 2003: 162)

A very useful publication on challenging behaviour in PCE from the (now defunct) Learning and Skills Development Agency describes types of challenging behaviour as:

- behaviour that disrupts routine teaching to an extent that challenges the teacher's resources and the concentration of other learners; this behaviour may not be violent, offensive or dangerous, simply disruptive
- behaviour that is offensive or violent, interfering with routine activity
- offending behaviour, including offending in the criminal sense, which bullies or ridicules fellow learners and creates an intimidating environment
- extreme passivity or non-engagement in learning
- intermittent patterns of attendance.

> (LSDA 2007: 2)

Thinking point: what behaviour challenges you?

Use the types of behaviour listed above to help with this activity.

- What range of challenging behaviours do you face as a teacher on a day-to-day basis?
- How do they affect you, the individuals concerned and your other students?
- How do you manage them?

Working with challenging behaviour

Strategy for survival: free to learn

This strategy returns to our definition at the start of the chapter, and is based on the commitment to ensuring that the freedom of all students to learn is not prejudiced through challenging behaviour. There will be varying degrees of severity associated with challenging behaviour, but there are some key strategies which can be used in all cases, and they are:

- *Establish rules* for appropriate behaviour, so that learning may take place (Wallace 2002: 39).

  The purpose of the rules is not to ensure compliance, but to ensure that everyone is safe and the best conditions for motivated learning are in place. Inflexible and punitive rules may well be counterproductive, although some breaking of the rules (particularly externally set rules) will at times involve sanctions or punishment. Your goal should be rules which are not excessive in number, which support learning and can be shared and agreed by your students.

- *Go to peace not war.* Our goals are to motivate students towards achievement, and celebrate that achievement, not to win a war with them.

  On many occasions through this book we have and will come across the philosophy that teachers are seeking to help their students to learn and achieve. This does not disappear because our students behave in ways we would prefer they don't. Of course some behaviour is genuinely a risk to you and other students, and we accept that appropriate action has to be taken for the safety and benefit of all. An environment which is conducive to learning for all is the goal for us all.

- *Stay together.* Make sure that your own teaching team and other colleagues (up to and including senior management) take a consistent and common approach.

  One thing which can make problems with behaviour more difficult to manage is when different people act differently in response to that behaviour. Training, risk assessment and communication are all essential components in making sure this doesn't happen. With some students, if they can find a weakness in your own collective way of working with them, they will certainly exploit it.

- *Analyse what's going on.* Gather information about why the behaviour is taking place, and plan what can be done to avoid, stop or change it.

  Where possible try to anticipate problems and prevent them happening, but also have in place clear procedures and strategies for dealing with them when they do happen. This may often involve information, advice and support from others such as learning support, health and safety and learning resources.

Specific actions

There are also actions you can take and questions you can ask which will make a difference, including:

- *Assess the potential risks and plan accordingly.* Risk assessments will result in clear courses of action.
- *Why is it happening?* What is the person's history, what triggers can produce the behaviour, how can the environment affect them?
- *What is it for?* Is this new or established behaviour, is it to gain attention?

- *What effect is it having?* Damage to property, personal injury, effect on others?
- *Applying the rules.* Remind all parties of the agreed rules, and apply them fairly and firmly.
- *Stop it.* Where risk is greatest, call for assistance or withdraw to minimise risk to you and others.
- *Defuse it.* Use diversionary activity to shift the behaviour into another mode.
- *Use available help.* Working with others is often more successful than working alone. Try to deploy peer/group pressure.
- *Review and make changes.* Review the actions you take and make changes to prevent or stop challenging behaviour on an ongoing basis.

Challenging behaviour examples

This section prompts you to plan how you could respond to occurrences of challenging behaviour in practice. Read each of the following brief examples. After the third is a list of strategies for managing potential or actual challenging behaviour. Try to match the strategies with the case studies. There are not necessarily exact matches in every case.

Kevin

Kevin has been excluded from school on numerous occasions on account of anti-social behaviour. His social skills and basic skills are poor, and he has already returned early from two spells of work experience in companies. He does enjoy 'hands on' work, and has helped his dad at home with some building projects. He can be volatile and disruptive, individually and in a group.

Wanda

Wanda is generally something of a non-conformist, both in dress and behaviour, who is studying AS levels, including psychology and English. When handing in her personal UCAS statement, she writes it in the form of a novel about her life, including some high-quality creative writing, alongside swearing and explicit sexual language.

Fighting in a workshop with tools (from Wallace 2002)

Two students start fighting in a practical workshop where you are teaching, using tools from that workshop.

Possible strategies

- Provide a training programme, including practical training, which can lead to a qualification using continuous assessment.
- Create an opportunity to discuss the behaviour openly, and consider the possible consequences.
- Get all other students to a safe place.

- Where intervention can be made safely, seek to calm things down.

- Discuss what to do with your course team and the relevant head of department.

- Ensure a high tutor/student ratio to maintain comprehensive support.

- Ensure appropriate reports/statements are produced as evidence.

- Organise integrated and student-centred support in life skills and basic skills.

- Call police and security.

- Agree on a number of possible courses of action, emphasising that the final choice (and the consequences) are the student's responsibility.

Expert advice

Paul Dix is a recognised expert on behaviour management, and he recognises the expert help he was given early on in his teaching career in schools, when other teachers showed him how to:

- Communicate my expectations to the students clearly

- Gain a perspective on my emotional state

- Empathise with students' individual needs

- Remain consistent and fair

- Manage confrontation and challenging conversations

- Use praise and positive reinforcement instead of constant sanctions

- Begin to build relationships with students who presented the full range of challenging behaviours

(Dix 2007: ix–x)

Expert advice will of course be valuable to you as a teacher on many occasions, but behaviour management can be the making or breaking of some teachers, so seeking out expert advice in this area can be particularly important.

Organisational behaviour management

As we have suggested, however, behaviour management is not just something for individual teachers or groups of teachers:

challenging behaviour should not be seen purely as a problem inherent in certain individuals but in the context of an inclusive learning approach where organisations do all they can to ensure that they create a learning environment that responds to the particular needs of all their learners. . . . this requires a whole-organisational approach that involves action at the levels of structure and systems as well as at delivery level.

(LSDA 2007: 31)

We appreciate that you, the teachers, are the ones often faced directly with challenging behaviour, but don't forget to remind your organisation if you need to that keeping all staff and learners safe is their responsibility too.

References

Catalyst Consulting Group (1999) *Accelerating Team Development: The Tuckman Model*. Capitola, CA: Catalyst Consulting Group.

Dix, P. (2007) *Taking Care of Behaviour: Practical Skills for Teachers*. Harlow: Pearson.

LSDA (2007) *What's Your Problem? Working with Learners with Challenging Behaviour*. London: LSDA.

Male, D. (2003) Challenging behaviour: the perceptions of teachers of children and young people with severe learning disabilities. *Journal of Research in Special Educational Needs*, 3: 162–171.

Tuckman, B. W. (1965) Developmental sequence in small groups. *Psychological Bulletin*, 63 (6): 384–399.

Wallace, S. (2002) *Managing and Motivating Students in Further Education*. Exeter: Learning Matters.

13

Putting the 'learning' into 'e-learning'

As we have discussed earlier in this book, we are living and working in a technologically advanced and information-rich world. This chapter is intended to help you make the most of the opportunities which e-learning can offer for you and your students, whilst highlighting the pitfalls which you will almost certainly encounter along the way. We begin with an explanation of what e-learning is in clear and simple language. You are then asked to complete the 'e-learning: enthusiast or sceptic quiz' about your attitude and approach to e-learning. The chapter then presents a strong argument for introducing simple but creative uses of e-learning into your teaching, emphasising the benefits for your students that it can bring. By following the advice in this chapter you should be able to enrich your students' learning and your teaching, and make sure that it is *learning* that is at the heart of e-learning.

What is e-learning?

The field of technology in education is a rapidly changing one, and definitions come and go almost as rapidly as new processors, screens and software. Terms which are used include 'educational technology', 'information and learning technology', 'online learning', 'learning technology', 'e-learning' and most recently 'technology-enhanced learning', which even has its own acronym of TEL. The most used terms have even changed somewhat in the relatively short time since the first edition of this book. All these terms have their own uses (and abuses) but the variety of terminology doesn't help in a field which can also be overhyped and misunderstood. We can, however, provide you with two terms and definitions which we feel work best. They are intended to be simple and comprehensive, to take account of current good practice and research, but mainly to be useful and relevant for you as teachers.

The first of these is *e-learning*. One well-respected definition put forward as part of the 'Waller–Wilson Matrix' is:

> E-Learning is the effective learning process created by combining digitally delivered content with (learning) support and services.
>
> (Waller and Wilson 2001: 1)

The DfES (2003) offered what on the face of it appeared to be a simple (if rather long) definition:

If someone is learning in a way that uses information and communication technologies (ICTs), they are using e-learning. They could be a pre-school child playing an interactive game; they could be a group of pupils collaborating on a history project with pupils in another country via the Internet; they could be geography students watching an animated diagram of a volcanic eruption their lecturer has just downloaded; they could be a nurse taking her driving theory test online with a reading aid to help her dyslexia – it all counts as e-learning.

(DfES 2003: 4)

For the purposes of this book, we will use a definition of e-learning provided by the Joint Information Services Committee (JISC), which is a well-respected national agency supporting educational uses of technology. This states that:

e-learning is learning facilitated and supported through the use of information and communications technology.

(JISC 2004: 10)

An essential element of this definition is the way it places learning at the heart of the process. One common mistake made in this area of teaching is to be seduced by the notion of what tends to be called 'putting the "e" into e-learning'. This is a valuable principle, but we have to be very careful to ensure that, in putting the 'e' in, we don't take the learning out!

The simple but authoritative JISC definition includes much more than using computers. If you use desktop and laptop computers; software, including assistive software; interactive whiteboards; digital cameras; mobile and wireless tools, including mobile phones; electronic communication tools, including email, discussion boards, chat facilities and video conferencing, Virtual Learning Environments (VLEs) or learning activity management systems – you are using e-learning (adapted from JISC 2004: 10).

A more recent and we believe very helpful addition to the acronym jungle in PCE is TEL or technology-enhanced learning. This term is not yet clearly defined, but JISC offers a contribution which we are happy to use:

the term 'technology-enhanced learning' . . . emphasises how technology adds value to learning.

(JISC 2009: 8)

It wasn't very long ago that many uses of technology seemed to be underpinned by the assumption that technology was the end in itself, not the means to an end. The definition above is part of a more widespread recognition that the technology on its own will probably not improve learning, but that it can enhance learning and add value to a considerable degree. If you have been teaching for some time, you probably came to that conclusion some time ago! It has just taken policy makers (and to a large degree researchers and theorists) somewhat longer to start to consider this as a positive way forward. So if you:

- use a social networking site, a digital voice recorder, an iPod or even an old tape recorder with your students to encourage them to develop their communication skills;
- show videos or pass around images or get students to draw images on laptops to help them understand and apply their learning;
- guide students in how to effectively use search engines

you are using technology-enhanced learning! You can probably think of many occasions when that has been the case, so you may be using technology to support learning more than you think.

Thinking point: enthusiast or sceptic quiz

Reflect on our deliberately broad definitions of e-learning and technology-enhanced learning, and think about your home, your workplace and where you spend the small amount of spare time which is left outside your working hours. Don't forget, a mobile phone, electronic till, cash machine, stereo, DVD and calculator all use ICT, as well as items mentioned earlier.

1 In a typical week, what technology do you use which could support learning?

2 How confident are you personally in using these technologies?

3 On a scale of 1–10, with 1 being a sceptic and 10 an enthusiast, where would you place yourself generally in relation to e-learning?

4 Which of these answers is closest to your views?

   a I have used e-learning successfully, and am convinced it is beneficial for student learning.

   b I get a buzz from using e-learning, and try to use it wherever I can in my teaching.

   c I have used e-learning, and will use it more, but need help and support.

   d When I try to use e-learning, things have a tendency to go wrong, which doesn't encourage me to use it more.

   e I'm not confident in my use of technology generally, and will avoid e-learning if I can.

   f E-learning is a waste of time, and I can get better results without it.

5 How much more do you expect to be using e-learning in your future teaching?

6 Does that prospect:

   a fill you with enthusiasm?

   b leave you unmoved?

   c fill you with dread?

This is by no means a scientific quiz, and you should easily be able to work out how much of an e-learning sceptic or enthusiast you are from your score. What it may also highlight are differences between your attitudes to teaching in general and those to e-learning in particular. Are you, for example, confident with using the gadgets and equipment you have at home and work, but reluctant to go along the e-learning route in your teaching, even though it may involve the same technology? Are you something of a technophobe generally, but would be delighted if someone would help you start off by teaching you how to use email?

Technology is the tool

E-learning is one of those areas of teachers' work which tend to generate extreme views, and much hype, but is it really worth bothering with? Haywood and Hutchins (2004) argue the positive case extremely well:

> Like any resource, ICT can be used creatively, to enhance learning. However, a learning activity does not have value simply because it is approached through a sophisticated technology. An activity which is educationally unsound and inappropriate for the student does not become a good learning experience simply because it is computer based. ICT can be used for impoverished as well as rich learning opportunities . . . It may be tempting to think 'why bother!' The reason for bothering is that ICT is a medium for developing a range of higher order skills including collaborative learning, collective thinking and building communities of students, whether local or global. It has the capacity to offer challenging and motivating opportunities, when students have access to powerful learning tools. Commercial games manufacturers have taken full advantage of this potential.
>
> (Haywood and Hutchins 2004: 8)

We would offer a slogan here which we hope makes our view as clear as possible:

> e-learning is the tool, but learning is the goal.

What works most often?

Is there then real evidence to show what works, and how you can try it out in your own teaching? Much has been written about the strengths and weaknesses of e-learning with general agreement that, despite significant investment over a large number of years, it is 'not embedded in our teaching and learning' (DfES 2003). More recently, Crawley (2009) offers a critique of the current state of progress, using nationally available data and reports from the key agencies and organisations involved in developing and promoting e-learning in PCE. His overall conclusion is not a positive one:

> If changes are not made to our current approaches, many more years of unfulfilled potential are likely and little sign of transformation. The potential of LT will never

be achieved as long as it is treated like a means to an end. The route to good learning generally involves good teaching, and no matter how sophisticated the technology becomes, that is unlikely to change.

(Crawley 2009: 45)

We are not suggesting that e-learning can't enhance teaching and learning. There is a good range of evidence from research which is positive about what can be achieved, and this tends to fit within the overall idea of technology-enhanced learning. The article cited above (Crawley 2009) also draws on a variety of authoritative sources to summarise some of these gains.

E-learning does work when:

- developments and implementations are taken forward in a step-by-step fashion, where the management, technical and teaching parts of an organisation work together in a planned manner, taking account of established good practice;
- national approaches and programmes are supported which take account of local circumstances and cultures, such as the 'ILT champions' scheme and the JISC Regional Support Centres;
- proper support for staff is available in implementing LT, and where they have access to training in both IT skills and using LT in teaching, and peer support in their use;
- technology is used as a clear and rapid means of communication between and among teachers and students, particularly through the use of email;
- the available richness of content and interactivity provided by technology to promote deeper learning is utilised;
- students and teachers are provided with opportunities to work at times and in places which are of their choosing;
- used in supporting students with a disability or learning difficulty;
- used in engaging hard-to-reach individuals and communities (adapted from Crawley 2009).

Many of these reflect what we have already argued about learning being centre stage, not the technology, so you may wish to try any of the above.

E-learning golden rules

However enthusiastic or sceptical you may be, there are some key golden rules you should always follow with e-learning, or even the above uses may be doomed to failure.

- Make sure you and your students have the IT skills needed to carry out any task or activity.
- Make sure using e-learning is appropriate and relevant.

- All the other aspects of your teaching need to be just as carefully and thoroughly prepared as usual.
- Make sure you have the equipment where and when you need it, and technical support available.
- Always have a plan B; at some stage, if it can go wrong, it will!

Trying out technology-enhanced learning

Now that we have defined TEL and provided ideas about ways in which it can enhance learning, this section provides a series of worked examples of how you can try it out in practice.

Photo gallery

Bring in a digital camera to use with a group of new students (making sure you have already checked they don't mind). Ask them to do the following things:

- Organise taking a photo of each student with which they are happy, then print them out, so that each photo is half an A4 page.
- Ask each person to write a mini-biography (50–100 words) without an identifying name, and get them all word-processed and printed out again on A5 paper.
- Ask the group to try to match the biographies to the photos, until you have all of them correct.

This can help build group identity, generate fun, develop writing, summarising and discussion skills, and familiarise your students with the use of digital cameras. It can be extended to form a pictorial progress review of the group over a period of time, and could develop towards making web pages, mini-books, social networks and presentations.

Find a forum

This task uses the Internet, and already existing online forums or discussion groups.

- Discuss with your group what their interests are, and locate online discussion groups or forums which cover those interests, for example football, pop music, films, soaps, local history.
- Ask small groups of students to select one forum or more to which they want to contribute.
- After checking the 'correct usage' rules of that forum, small groups write contributions which will start a new line of discussion, and enter them on to the forum.
- Each group then monitors the responses over a period of time, and time is set aside for a verbal summary to a whole group discussion about the results.

This activity can develop skills in responsible Internet use, verbal discussion, writing to criteria, and extending of expertise and understanding in the field of their interest. It can be extended into specially designed groups which are solely for your student group, and which can become part of your assessment of their knowledge and understanding.

How does it work?

You need to take a group of motor vehicle students through the process of how a car engine works. You have a workshop with a real engine, and cars, some of which work, but it has always been difficult to really get this topic over. There are various resources which can show you this in other ways, and one of the best is the 'how stuff works' web site, which includes animations, cutaway diagrams and detailed explanations at no charge. You will easily be able to locate this site and others which are similar through a simple search on the Internet.

- Find a source which will help to put your topic over to your students effectively, and carefully plan how to use it.
- Get organised to project the web pages live to your students via a projector.
- Make sure that you check out any difficult to understand or less effective parts in advance, then run your presentation, using the parts which have most visual impact (e.g. diagrams and animations).
- Build other learning activities around the source to help the students when they are visiting the site themselves as backup for your presentation.

This can provide a high-quality resource at no cost, and can bring things to the students which they cannot otherwise experience in one place. Giving students responsibility for finding other sources and sharing them with their peers can be a strong motivator, and can build a pool of resources for the benefit of all.

Virtual tourism

Ever visited one of those holiday villa web sites which give you a 'virtual tour' of the properties you would like to stay in? It's now possible to let your students be 'virtual tourists' in many ways through the power of technology. You can visit places and situations which are impossible or impractical to experience in any other way, and bring them alive for your students. Virtual tours you can easily find include:

- Shakespeare's Globe Theatre in London;
- the NASA space shuttle;
- No. 10 Downing Street;
- a front-line trench during the First World War.

You have to of course be careful that there is a point to using such resources, but the growing power and speed of current computers can bring many animations, simulations and other resources to your and your students' desktops.

We hope these examples of moving on to the virtual wheel of learning have whetted your appetites enough for you to get into putting the learning into e-learning, but just make sure that, when you do, you remember to think about how it actually worked, and what benefits there were. Always ask:

- What benefits did your students get from using e-learning?
- Did you notice improvements in student involvement, motivation and results in comparison with the use of other learning tools?
- What would you do differently next time?
- Overall was it worth it for you and your students?

References

Crawley, J. (2009) Much technology, but limited impact: what progress has been made with Learning Technology in the Post Compulsory Education (PCE) sector? *Teaching in Lifelong Learning*, 1 (1): 43–50.

DfES (2003) *Towards a Unified e-Learning Strategy*. Consultation Document. London: DfES.

Haywood, S. and Hutchins, M. (2004) ICT and learning for the future. In Ward, S. (ed.) *Education Studies: A Student's Guide*. London: Routledge.

JISC (2004) *Effective Practice with e-Learning*. Bristol: JISC.

JISC (2009) *Effective Practice in a Digital Age: A Guide to Technology-Enhanced Learning and Teaching*. Bristol: JISC.

Waller, V. and Wilson, J. (2001) A definition for e-learning. *Open and Distance Learning Quality Council (ODL QC) Newsletter* October:1–2.

Surviving outside the classroom

14

Working with colleagues

This first chapter in Part IV concentrates on the other people you work with inside your organisation, starting with a summary of some of the most common *job roles and responsibilities* which exist in PCE *other than teachers*. The chapter then moves on to the theme of personality traits, and how people in organisations interact with each other in interesting and challenging ways. The chapter closes by considering how to contribute to the building of effective teams. By the end of the chapter, surviving working with your colleagues should become less of a challenge.

Who are your colleagues?

The diversity of PCE includes a wide range of jobs and, given the variety of 'learning sites' at which provision operates, it is difficult to generalise about the type of teaching or non-teaching colleagues you will be working with. At one end of the scale you may be part of a department in a large further education college. Over 100 teaching staff may be employed by that department, 60 of whom are full-time, and your immediate circle of teaching and non-teaching colleagues could be 50 or more in size. At the other end of the scale, if you are a part-time aromatherapy, literacy or French teacher, who teaches only during the evening in community venues for two to three hours per week and at the most 30 weeks of the year, your immediate colleagues may be the caretaker, the person teaching in the room next door, and the security person or key holder! Certain functions do, however, tend to be present in all but the smallest organisations in PCE and most teachers will have contact with them. Brief descriptions of some of those most common functions follow.

Student support

Exactly what is student support will vary from one organisation to another, but this area of work is generally focussed on providing individual students and groups of students with assistance related to their learning. Generally the assistance helps students to join, stay on and achieve in learning programmes, and staff providing student support are extremely important in making the difference between achievement and under-achievement in many cases. They often work directly with the teaching team, so can be some of the closest colleagues you will have.

Student support involves:

- providing specialist support staff to work directly (often one to one) with students in and outside their sessions, according to the particular needs of those students;

- organising and providing advice and guidance services for prospective, current and past students including course information, careers advice, counselling and pastoral care;

- monitoring and supporting attendance by, and progress of, students on programmes;

- early identification of, and support for, students who may be 'at risk' in various ways of dropping out;

- providing and coordinating facilities for students to make use of enrichment activities and social facilities;

- providing information about and referral to other organisations, programmes and staff who can assist students when in difficulty.

Learning resources

Another important group of staff are those who organise, monitor the use of and make available the learning resources of the organisation for students and staff. This can include information professionals in a library or learning resource centre, learning technologists who support the development of online services and e-learning, and many more.

Their work generally involves:

- managing and operating a lending system for books and other loan items;

- training staff and students in the location and use of learning resources, study skills, information skills and specialist electronic services;

- identifying and locating resources for staff in requested areas;

- managing bookings for computers and Internet facilities, and overseeing facilities such as virtual learning environments;

- maintaining a suitable study environment for students in learning resource centres;

- working with staff to create learning resources for their teaching.

Facilities, technical support and administration

Without this group of staff, organisations would quickly grind to a halt irrespective of the quality of the teachers. Without receptionists, technicians, caretakers, canteen staff, security and maintenance the buildings would be cold, closed and dirty, and the students hungry, uncomfortable and untidy. With e-learning in particular, technical support is as important as the content and style of the learning programmes. If you can't get online or your projector doesn't work, you can't e-learn! At their best, these staff can provide creative and essential contributions to the teaching and learning of any organisation. Their activities include:

- opening and securing the organisation's learning sites;
- maintaining buildings, grounds, equipment and rooms;
- dealing with telephone enquiries, writing reports and correspondence, staffing reception and many other areas;
- helping staff solve technical problems.

Thinking point: not the teacher

What is likely to be the common factor in the answers to all these questions?

- When prospective students contact your organisation, who is likely to be the first person they speak to?
- As a student arrives at your organisation for the first time, what is going to make the first impression on them?
- If a student has a problem with a computer in the learning resources centre, who will be available to help?
- If a student isn't sure where their class is, who will tell them?
- When a student passes their qualification, who gets the certificate to them?

The answer to all these questions is almost certainly 'not the teacher'. Does that help you to realise how important everyone else in the organisation other than teachers actually is?

Personality traits

As we have indicated throughout the book, PCE works with a great range and diversity of students. It also employs an almost equally diverse body of staff, ranging from conventionally 'academic' trained professional teachers, vocational specialists who have moved from industry to teaching, past students who move into teaching after being students, and people who are working in other jobs whilst teaching part-time. Add to that the range of people who work in the sector who are not teaching but doing other jobs within teaching organisations, and you get an interesting mixture!

We already looked at group dynamics in Chapter 12 as one way of understanding how different people interact, and how that can be managed as a teacher. When it comes to the teachers, group dynamics are equally important, and you could use that understanding of the stages of group development when working with other teachers. Another way is to consider the *personality traits* of any group of staff, or their individual personality differences. Personality types and how they work together are a major concern in organisational and management development, but it is a field in which it is easy to become buried under test results, questionnaires, analysis and complications. The following example is an approach to personality which we feel is accessible and clear, but based on sound theory.

The five-factor model of personality

In the field of personality types, the five-factor model, as it is called, has a range of admirers. Two of the key writers to define its properties are McCrae and Costa (1996), and they argue that the factors are not fixed points, but points on a scale, with many people falling between the extremes. Your place on the scale is believed to stay stable through much of adult life, so it should be possible to make use of this approach to understand behaviour over an extended period of time.

The five factors are:

1. Extraversion

Extraverts tend to be more physically and verbally active, whereas introverts are independent, reserved and steady and like being alone. The person in the middle of the dimension likes a mix between social situations and solitude. Extraverts are adventurous, assertive, frank, sociable and talkative. Introverts are quiet, reserved, shy and unsociable.

IMPACT ON THE WORKPLACE

Extraverts are felt to be communicative, visioning and ready to engage in interpersonal relations, qualities which should be useful in leaders or potential leaders. Introverts may function effectively within a supportive group, but could find regular face-to-face contact with students and staff challenging. A large proportion of either in a workplace would be a problem.

2. Agreeableness

Agreeable personalities tend to be good-natured, caring, sympathetic and forgiving. Disagreeable people are indifferent, self-centred, jealous and rude.

IMPACT IN THE WORKPLACE

If your workplace were peopled with people on the disagreeable end of the scale (particularly if they are managers!), this would have a highly negative impact, as they would be likely to pressure and coerce others. Agreeable traits would contribute to an emotionally positive environment, and could contribute significantly in terms of teamwork and flexibility or 'give and take'.

3. Conscientiousness

The conscientious person is focussed, reliable, well organised, self-disciplined and careful. The slacker is impulsive, unreliable, easy to put off and lacking in organisation.

IMPACT IN THE WORKPLACE

The conscientious are in many ways, as the name suggests, the 'conscience' of the organisation, who are likely to promote ethics and values, whilst putting in consistent effort, and being ready to work with others. Slackers are probably the biggest burden any organisation carries.

4. Neuroticism

Those with a tendency towards neuroticism are more worried, temperamental, insecure and prone to sadness. Emotionally stable personalities are calm, stable and relaxed.

IMPACT ON THE WORKPLACE

Stress in the workplace can breed neuroticism, and can plunge those who are not generally nervous into bouts of worrying, hesitancy and disengagement from their work. Neurotics can become detached and distant from their co-workers and their workplace. Promoting emotional stability, the other end of this scale, should be a central concern of all workplaces, and can strongly foster teamwork, productivity and efficiency.

5. Openness

People with high openness have broader interests, and are complex, liberal, creative and curious. Those who are more closed tend to be conventional, uncreative, have narrow interests and avoid new experiences.

IMPACT ON THE WORKPLACE

Those who are open will be the thinkers, visioners and creative forces at work but will also be sensitive to the internal and external context they are working in. The closed thinkers may well, however, see openness as dangerous and difficult to manage so can be troubled by 'too much' openness.

Using the five factors

When you look at these descriptions, you will naturally start rating yourself and the people you work with and know. The results you come up with will inevitably be affected by how honest you are, and how much you are prepared to admit some of your less attractive personality traits. The simple activity which follows will help you identify where you and selected others fit on the five-factor model.

Thinking point: the five-factor quiz – what are you like? (Table 14.1)

- Use your initials, and mark where you think you are on the matrix for each personality trait, working through all five factors.

- Join the points together into a continuous line, to see your profile.

- Add ratings for at least two other people in your organisation, one of whom should be the senior manager.

The overall profile will give you some significant insights into the mix of personalities in your organisation, and can be really revealing if you profile all of your team. The factors on the left are generally considered to be more positive than those on the right, but that doesn't necessarily mean a workplace full of people with profiles along the left hand side will necessarily be the most productive and effective. It is possible to get a good indication of the balance of personalities in your team from a profiling exercise such as this. There are no hard and fast rules about which personality traits must be mixed together, so we strongly advise using such profiles as indicators only.

From personalities to a working team

Using the matrix, you can identify the personality traits of as many of your working colleagues as you wish. If you are an open, conscientious, agreeable and emotionally stable extrovert who is surrounded by closed, disorganised, disagreeable and neurotic introverts, you are probably somewhat scared! Equally, if you were surrounded by people who all have the same personality traits as you, would that work? The key challenge for you and your organisation is to make the best use of the different personality types available to produce a balanced team. Teams can still work effectively despite containing apparently incompatible personalities, just as much as teams can be ineffective despite appearing to have the perfect blend of personalities. The crucial message is that:

TABLE 14.1 The five-factor quiz – what are you like?

FACTOR	RATING							FACTOR
	3	2	1	0	1	2	3	
Extraversion								Introversion
Agreeableness								Disagreeableness
Emotional stability								Neuroticism
Conscientiousness								Slackness
Openness								Closedness

effective teamwork is at the centre of any successful organisation.

A major research project into team working in the UK National Health Service operated over a three-year period and involved 400 teams, 7,000 NHS personnel and a 'large number' of NHS clients. The report on this research, from the Aston Centre for Health Service Organisation Research (2000), makes some significant points about teamwork. Mohrman and Cohen's definition of a team (Mohrman *et al.* 1995: 3) is used, which describes it as:

> a group of individuals who work together to produce products or deliver services for which they are mutually accountable. Team members share goals and are mutually held accountable for meeting them, they are interdependent in their accomplishment, and they affect the results through their interactions with one another. Because the team is held collectively accountable, the work of integrating with one another is included among the responsibilities of each member.

This model of teamwork is highly relevant to PCE, and the conclusions of the research emphasise a number of characteristics of effectively functioning teams. We have used those characteristics to inform our own 'dream team checklist'.

Dream team checklist

Teams work effectively when:

- providing a high-quality service is the key motivating factor;
- innovation is encouraged;
- people from different disciplines have opportunities to work together;
- objectives are clear;
- participation by team members is high;
- meetings and communication are regular and clear.

The benefits for the team, its members and the organisation include:

- clearer leadership;
- more effective team processes;
- innovation and improvements in the quality of service;
- reduced stress for team members;
- wider benefits for all including increased morale, confidence and autonomy.

Strategy for survival: picking your dream team

Reflecting on the personality traits of the people in your organisation, and considering the checklist above, use this activity to develop your 'dream team'. Bear in mind you probably don't have the power to change the personalities, so this is about using teamwork to overcome differences and accentuate positives.

- Identify two ways where your own team is working effectively and two where it is not.

- Identify two ways where the organisation as a team is working effectively and two where it is not.

- Decide on an area where you believe you have some capacity to change the situation for the better.

- Write down two actions you will take to improve team working over the next month.

- Get team working!

- Make sure to check in a month to see how it worked out.

References

Aston Centre for Health Service Organisation Research (2000) *Healthcare Team Effectiveness Project.* Birmingham: Aston University.

McCrae, P. R. and Costa, P. T. (1996) Toward a new generation of personality theories: theoretical contexts for the Five-Factor model. In Wiggins, J. S. (ed.) *The Five-Factor Model of Personality: Theoretical Perspectives.* New York: Guilford Press.

Mohrman, S. A., Cohen, S. G. and Mohrman, A. M. Jr (1995) *Designing Team-Based Organisations.* San Francisco: Jossey-Bass.

15

Working under pressure and managing conflict

This chapter takes a look at two related areas which teachers in PCE have often said they are least prepared for: a workload and working situation which puts them under intense pressure, and managing conflict which may arise outside the classroom. We start by explaining what we are calling the 'three Ps', paper pressure, people pressure and personal pressure. The chapter then emphasises how important it is to learn to stay calm and be positive, remembering there is more to life than work alone. Focussed advice on ways of prioritising and managing time follows, and then an introduction to what can cause conflict, and some basic techniques for managing conflict situations.

Paper pressure, people pressure and personal pressure

Most of the aspects of pressure fall under what we call the 'three Ps', and you need to remember they are not necessarily always negative types of pressure.

Paper pressure

We may be in an electronic age, but the mountain of paper which can pile up on a teacher's desk during just one week is at times quite staggering. Add to this the 'electronic paper' (i.e. the items which arrive in your inbox, for example, rather than as hard copy), and you really do have paper pressure. Even deciding whether to print the electronic paper adds further pressure. A typical selection could include:

- *paper for your teaching* – documentation directly related to your teaching (e.g. schemes of work, session plans, handouts, presentations, assessment tasks, assignment briefs);
- *paper for your students* – student support publications/documentation (e.g. organisational handbooks for your course, from other departments, promoting services for students);
- *paper for your learning programmes* – the syllabus or curriculum you are working with (e.g. one of the guides to the 14–19 diplomas is a 7.6 megabyte download and runs to 304 pages);

- *paper from inside* – internal communications (e.g. notes/memos from colleagues, staff circulars, minutes of meetings, policies, procedures);
- *paper from outside* – external communications (e.g. awarding body communications, reports, policy documents, notifications of meetings, staff development).

This does not even include other important paper pressures, such as marking student work, or reading, research or investigation you may wish to carry out. Paper pressure is so intense that we shall deal with it in more detail in a later chapter.

People pressure

People pressure is about the feelings, issues and complications which can arise when you are interacting with or responding to other people, sometimes out of choice, but not always. The people who have been significant contributors to your particular paper mountain can often be part of the pressure, but they are by no means the only people involved. At least with paper pressure you can find a quiet (or at least quieter) corner to read all the paper. But with people pressure you often need to sort it out face to face. The electronic age has made email contact much more common, but there are people pressures associated even with electronic communication, as there tends to be an inbuilt expectation of a rapid response. People pressure can come from:

- students who wish to be seen outside of teaching/tutorial time;
- colleagues wishing to work collaboratively with you on something of mutual interest;
- external enquiries, liaison and contacts such as telephone calls or being present at publicity or recruitment events;
- managers who expect you to be available to see them at any time;
- sudden unexpected situations with any of the above.

Personal pressure

Personal pressure is about how you as a person receive, process and deal with all of the pressures involved in your life and work. Essentially, you are the person at the heart of all of this, so you need to develop your own ways of dealing with it, and recognising the impact on yourself, your colleagues, friends and family.

If you are working to help other people, knowing yourself well is crucial.

The earlier content on personality traits and group dynamics should help here, but pause briefly for this next thinking point, to reflect on how you personally recognise and manage pressure.

Thinking point: recognising the three Ps

With a friend or colleague, make a list of the most persistent paper, people and personal pressures you face in your work as a teacher. Group them under the different types as headings if that helps. Try to answer these questions:

- What strategies for dealing with pressure do you use generally, and how well do they work?
- Choosing one of the most persistent pressures, how effectively do you manage it?
- Do you find any one of the three Ps more difficult than the others?
- What other strategies can you try to reduce pressure?

Calm down! Be positive!

It has been argued that being able to stay calm and think positively can help with managing most problems and issues in life, and we would generally endorse that view. From thinkers and philosophers such as Ghandi and Carl Rogers, and from non-violent protests to therapeutic relationships, emphasis is given to what we would describe as 'active calmness'. This is not a state of passive acquiescence, but rather more positively charged calmness, which is a combination of relaxed self-awareness and positive thinking. How can we work to achieve active calmness, when there are so many pressures surrounding us?

Strategy for survival: calm down

Relaxing in pressured situations is by definition difficult, as there are both physical (hormones released in stressful situations can make us physically feel we need to run away) and psychological (various reactions, ranging from being ill at ease to panic attacks) factors involved. Keeping those feelings and reactions at bay is possible, however, and some simple techniques to use are:

- *Pause and count to ten*. The age-old technique of stopping for a brief period of time and thinking before reacting gives pause for thought and can make a real difference.
- *Action replay*. Run through the pressures which are making you anxious and ask yourself, 'are they really as bad as I thought they were?'
- *Buffer zone*. Make sure you have activities (e.g. hobbies, friends and family, travel, reading novels) which are nothing to do with work to take you away from your pressure sources, and give you a zone to learn to relax.

> ■ *Fit for purpose.* If you are unhealthy, unfit and run down, you will find keeping calm even more difficult. Find a simple starting point to making yourself more 'fit for purpose', such as taking breaks even if they are only five minutes long, or walking more instead of using the car.

Strategy for survival: be positive

In terms of working with pressure, being positive is all about not getting 'weighed down' by the pressures at every stage, and can also help what we have called being 'actively critical' earlier in the book. Much of this is about mindsets, but it is possible to move away from being negative if you are prepared to try to make some changes in the way you think about pressures. You can remain positive by:

challenging demanding musts, shoulds, have tos, oughts and got tos.

Just stop and question some of those immediate and perhaps understandable negative thoughts and responses. Is the latest deadline as real as my head is telling me? Is my thinking about the deadline helpful or stress-inducing? Where is my thinking getting me?

■ Challenging 'awfulising' beliefs:

Is it really going to be awful if I don't achieve the deadline or goal? Will it really be the end of the world? Am I turning a 'life hassle' into a 'life horror'? Am I making a mountain out of a molehill?

■ Challenging 'I can't stand it-itis':

Will I really fall apart and not be able to stand the outcome? Surely I'm living proof that I've survived not reaching deadlines on previous occasions?

■ Challenging global ratings of the self or others:

Is it fair to rate myself (or others) globally as a total failure if I've failed to accomplish one task?

Using this approach to positive thinking means that thoughts like 'If I don't make that deadline it would be awful, and I'd be a failure' become 'If I failed to reach the deadline on this occasion, I just failed to reach the deadline – that's all. I have done my best and I will do my best with the next deadline' (adapted from Clow and Palmer 2004).

Prioritising and managing time

Once you have achieved 'active calm' and established positive thoughts, not very much is going to change if your workload is so high that you still have far more to do than can possibly be done in the time you have available to do it. Not only that, over-work is guaranteed to make your feelings of calm rapidly disappear! There are some simple routines and approaches to managing your time which can genuinely make a difference, but there is one key requirement, without which not much will change.

You need to master the art of saying 'no'.

This does not mean being the 'awkward squad', and it does not mean you are not committed to your job and your students. It means you wish to operate in a positive, effective and efficient manner and that you are prepared to firmly and assertively explain why you can't always do everything. Don't forget that stress reduces your performance so it is not in anyone's interest for you to work 25 hours a day.

Strategy for survival: bin it!

This can be a really helpful way of prioritising, and is based on taking limited risks with what you decide to prioritise. You need to be brave, and to pause and think about work before you get started on it.

■ As work comes in, create three piles, the 'do it', 'leave it' and 'bin it' piles. (Even if the work isn't on paper, writing the task down and putting it on one of these piles helps.)

Don't actually bin anything at this stage.

■ Do the 'do it' tasks first, then the 'leave it' tasks.

■ The first few times, don't do the 'bin it' tasks for a short time, and see if they return to haunt you. If not, simply don't do the 'bin it' tasks.

■ If you feel uncomfortable with binning it, experiment with moving items temporarily from the 'bin it' to the 'leave it' pile and see what happens.

Time management matrix

A more gentle and perhaps less risky way of planning your time is what tends to be called a 'time management' matrix' (Figure 15.1). Stephen Covey (1990) produced such a tool, and the overall idea is to place items in the matrix based on how 'important' or 'not important' they are on one dimension, and how 'urgent' or 'not urgent' they are along the other. Figure 15.1 illustrates the four quadrants of the matrix, and suggests some of the items which may be placed in each quadrant.

	URGENT	NOT URGENT
IMPORTANT	**QUADRANT 1** Crises Pressing problems Deadlines	**QUADRANT 2** Exploiting new opportunities Building relationships Planning Reviewing Recreation
NOT IMPORTANT	**QUADRANT 3** Interruptions Some phone calls / emails Some meetings	**QUADRANT 4** Trivia Some phone calls / emails Some meetings Wastes of time Task avoidance

FIGURE 15.1 Time management matrix.

Covey (1990: 3) argues 'Quadrant 2 is the heart of effective personal management. It deals with things that are not urgent, but are important.' By planning to spend more time in Quadrant 2, we can take another look at workload and priorities, and create solutions that, over time, reduce the quantity and urgency of items typically found in Quadrants 1 and 3.

Strategy for survival: reloading the matrix

- Complete your own version of the time management matrix, at the same time as one other person completes their own.

- Select two items from Quadrant 2, and agree with your partner that you will give them more time over the next two weeks. This is your *time management contract*.

- Get together again in two weeks (time permitting of course!) and honour the contract. Having to report on your changes to someone else reduces the chance of you finding excuses not to do it.

Understanding conflict and managing conflict situations

John Crawley, who has written extensively on conflict management, defines conflict as 'a manifestation of differences working against one another' (Crawley 1992: 10). He goes on to argue that conflicts can 'explode', and the components which make them explosive are:

- *ingredients* – the differences which are present between people, including age, gender, values, beliefs, status and behaviours;
- *combinations and conditions* – the contacts between people, and the structures and environment in which they live and work;
- *the spark* – the clash of differences;
- *the burning fuse* – circumstances and feelings which can slowly ignite the conflict such as defensiveness, power games and inability to find a resolution;
- *the explosion* – a dramatic, violent exchange which affects the people nearby as well as those directly involved.

We will have probably all experienced 'explosive' conflicts, either at work or at home, and resolving them once they have become explosive can be exceptionally difficult, and can also involve emotional, material and financial costs. There are therefore wide gains to be made by reducing and managing conflict.

Managing conflict effectively promotes positive personal interactions, but can also be efficient and cost-effective.

Cooperative (win/win) conflict

How then can we avoid explosions of conflict? 'Conflicts need not always turn out this way. Constructive conflict management will enable you to transform the interaction.' (Crawley 1992: 10). This approach sees conflict as a shared problem to be solved by collaborative effort, in which all parties have something to gain. This recognises all parties' interests as legitimate, and seeks a solution which is responsive to the needs of all. The approach is more concerned with looking for ways forward, solving problems and creating more effective working relationships, rather than settling arguments about right and wrong or attributing blame.

Managing conflict using this problem-solving style means you need to:

- see big problems as a series of smaller problems, and tackle them a little at a time;
- evaluate the impact of possible solutions as you explore them;
- collect background information about the problem and the expectations and needs of all involved;
- get people to say how they see things, how they feel and what they want rather than labelling or blaming;
- get some agreement about action, and keep on track with the action;

- take it steadily (e.g. do not rush into solutions);
- keep working even when things are getting tough.

Conflict situations

Three brief descriptions follow of potentially explosive conflict situations which you may come across outside the classroom. Think about how you could stop that happening, using some of the approaches we have presented so far. Some suggestions will appear at the end of the section.

Feedback from the boss

Your immediate boss has recently changed, and the new person rarely gives you positive feedback about your work, tending to pick out and emphasise small problems. He has interrupted you in meetings and postponed supervision sessions with you, and your overall impression is that your work is not valued highly.

Chalk and cheese

Two of your colleagues, who have spaces in the office you all share with six other staff, just do not get on with each other. One has been working for the organisation for 22 years and is 46, and the other for just six months and is 23. They have different views about many things, but both teach the same subject. When working together they regularly make negative comments about each other, and they have been heard having heated discussions out in the corridor by the office, which usually end with one or the other stomping off aggrieved.

Team not working

A group of eight staff who work together have not gelled as a team, despite all working effectively as individuals in their own roles. When the group comes together, a tense atmosphere exists, and, when they need to work cooperatively to implement a new initiative, progress is slow and uncomfortable. When they meet others in the organisation they tend to make negative comments about other members of the team.

Thinking point: avoiding explosions

All of these above situations are 'smouldering', and we want to stop them sparking into explosive conflict. Here are some strategies which could work. Match the strategies to the situations where you think they could work.

- Bring in others to work with the people in conflict as mediators. Take care about who is approached.
- Encourage the parties to the conflict to come together in groups, and give them a chance to talk.

- Make positive use of time with your boss, be assertive and clarify expectations and understandings. Do you each know clearly what the other expects?

- Respond positively to challenges by being 'actively calm'.

- Get information about differences between parties in a conflict quickly to clarify what is going on.

- Ensure everyone is listened to but encourage them to listen as well.

- Look for small improvements which all can accept to move forward.

Making these adjustments can have a major impact on reducing conflict.

References

Clow, A. and Palmer, S. (2004) *The Stress Test*. London: BBC.

Covey, S. (1990) *The Seven Habits of Highly Effective People*. New York: Simon & Schuster.

Crawley, John (1992) *Constructive Conflict Management: Managing to Make a Difference*. London: Nicholas Brierly Publishers.

Mohrman, S. A., Cohen, S. G. and Mohrman, A. M. Jr (1995) *Designing Team-Based Organisations*. San Francisco: Jossey-Bass.

16

Are you teaching in a learning organisation?

This chapter starts by considering just what a 'learning organisation' is, and how they fit into our 'knowledge age' and the world of PCE. Checking how your organisation rates as a learning organisation follows, together with some ideas about organisational culture and the way that can affect the day-to-day business of teaching and learning. The chapter concludes with a consideration of how power can operate in the smallest or the largest organisations, and some strategies for keeping that power on your side.

Learning organisations in the knowledge age

Much has been written and said on 'learning organisations', but just how much this is an ideal notion of an organisation and how much it is a reality can sometimes be difficult to judge. When organisations are operating in a climate of pressure, and results are important, operating as a learning organisation could be seen to be of very much secondary importance, and even something of a luxury. In a rapidly changing, technologically sophisticated world, operating as a learning organisation is not so much a luxury as a necessity. Peter Senge has been influential in this area. His view is that learning organisations are:

> organisations where people continually expand their capacity to create the results they truly desire, where new and expansive patterns of thinking are nurtured, where collective aspiration is set free, and where people are continually learning to see the whole together.
>
> (Senge 1990: 3)

This vision could be seen as somewhat idealistic, but the emphasis on the value of teamwork and learning together is really important. Charles Handy has a typically clear and accessible contribution to this theme:

> the learning organisation can mean two things – it can mean an organisation which learns and/or an organisation which encourages learning in its people. It should mean both.
>
> (Handy 1995: 179)

Any organisation which does not pay careful attention to the processes and interactions between its workers, and see them as a developing and learning team, is not just out of date; it is foolish. Working towards common goals which at least in part overlap with individual goals is essential for most of us, whether we are building cars, helping our workmates, nursing the elderly or teaching. The gains and positive benefits of working together in a shared atmosphere of learning are economic, social and personal, and after all:

if an organisation which has teaching as its core business cannot try to be a learning organisation, we may as well all give up and go home.

Thinking point: is yours a learning organisation?

The statements in Table 16.1 reflect current thinking on the characteristics of a learning organisation. Rate your organisation against each statement from 1 to 4 (1 is low and 4 is high).

The maximum score here is 100. If you scored 40 or below, your organisation is in trouble!

Organisational culture

Organizational culture is the set of, often unconsciously held, beliefs, ideas, knowledge and values which shape the way things happen and makes some courses of action unthinkable. An organization's culture therefore determines, to a large extent, its capacity for solving problems.

(Bate 1994: 224)

Organisational culture is manifested almost as soon as you get anywhere near any organisation, and can have a major impact not just on whether the organisation is a learning organisation, but on all aspects of what the organisation does and stands for. It is not of course the only thing which affects how an organisation works, as where you are situated geographically, the resources you have at your disposal, your relative size and financial position, to name a few, all have an impact. Changing organisational culture can be enormously difficult, however, partly because it tends to start at the top of the organisation, and partly because we are not in an environment which provides much time and space for thinking about organisational culture, and how to change or improve it.

TABLE 16.1 Is yours a learning organisation?

ORGANISATIONAL AREA	RATING (1–4)
Organisational dynamics	
We are encouraged to manage our own learning and development	
A positive listening and feedback environment exists	
Training is available in how to learn	
Teams and individuals use the wheel of learning to reflect and act on their own learning	
Teachers are supported to take a strategic approach	
The organisation's approach to change and development	
Senior managers accept the idea of a learning organisation	
There is a climate which supports the idea of learning	
We learn from our weaknesses and our achievements	
Opportunities to learn are part of day-to-day business	
There is a flat management structure which promotes communication and learning at all levels	
Empowerment of people	
The workforce is empowered to work and learn	
Authority is delegated and decentralised	
Managers have a facilitative, mentoring approach	
We share with other organisations to improve our and their service	
We participate in joint learning events with other relevant PCE stakeholders	
Managing knowledge	
We benchmark our best practices against others and seek to learn from them	
Training and support is available for staff in innovation and creative thinking	
Trialling and evaluating new areas of work is embedded in our practice	
We and others are able to make use of our accumulated knowledge in our field	
We share that knowledge systematically and on an ongoing basis with others	
Technological support	
Our uses of technology clearly benefit our key purpose	
Staff and students have ready access to the Internet and other learning technology	
Technology-enhanced learning is embedded in our practice	
We make use of e-learning within our curriculum	
We make use of technology to support our evaluation and development systems	
Total score (out of 100)	

Thinking point: the 'walkabout audit' – testing the organisational culture

Try a 'walkabout audit' where you just walk around any organisation involved in PCE. What do these comments from walkabout audits tell you about the culture of the organisations involved?

- You walk in the gates of your local college. What you first see is a mixture of older and newer buildings. They all appear well looked after, and the site is really clean, with flower beds providing splashes of colour to greet you. Along the drive and footpaths there are well-positioned pieces of student work, including sculptures, displays and murals. You can find your way to reception easily.

- You arrive for an evening class in a small rural learning centre. It's midwinter outside, but a warm coffee bar is sited just as you go in, and you join a small group of students who are already seated chatting before starting their classes. The centre administrator is welcoming all arrivals, and passing round copies of next year's prospectus of classes, and a leaflet on some new computer training.

- You arrive at one of the campuses of a college you are considering attending full-time. The buildings are run down, and finding the right building is extremely hard, as there are either no signs or broken signs. To get into the building, you have to go through a group of people smoking outside the door, and when you get inside, there is no receptionist and no clear signs showing where to go. You wait at reception for several minutes before anyone asks you what you want, and then wait 20 minutes to see someone.

Isn't that first impression powerful? We discussed the more general aspects of working with colleagues in an earlier chapter, but just ask yourself the question: where would you rather learn or work out of the examples above? The examples show well that

organisational culture is physically invisible, but you will see its effects everywhere.

If culture is so pervasive, what can we do to change or improve it? Because organisational culture is mainly a shared concept, people can sometimes feel their capacity to make any change is limited, and a feeling of helplessness can result.

Any one member of an organisation can influence and change the culture of that organisation by making 'choices for change'.

Strategy for survival: choices for change

When you are under pressure, you may feel it is difficult to get involved in changing the culture of your organisation. You've done the learning organisation rating, and the organisation does badly. There are ways to get involved in trying to change negative aspects of the organisation's culture, but you must wholeheartedly engage with the positive aspects. Here are some suggestions of 'choices for change' you could make.

- The Internet café in your organisation is a much more pleasant place to meet colleagues and actually relax than the general canteen. Arrange to have a meeting with your team manager there, and ask them to think about how they feel it compares with the canteen.

- You have found a really good web site, which you think is worth everyone in your subject team using. Organise a lunchtime demo of the site, and provide coffee and cakes to give your team a 'hands-on' taste of the web site.

- Sit in your reception area, and watch people arriving for appointments or as visitors. How long do they have to wait, how are they dealt with, and how comfortable and confident do they look? Make some notes and report back on it to your next departmental meeting, asking for comments.

- Do a 'walkabout audit': take a digital camera out around your site, capturing the best and worst bits. Show both to your boss, your colleagues and your students, and ask them what they can do to make things better.

These are all very small steps, but

you can help change to happen, so grasp the opportunity.

Power and influence

As a teacher in an organisation, whether a small or large one, you both have power, and are affected by power, in a variety of ways. Organisations, their cultures, systems and processes, and the way they develop can change dramatically depending on the power relationships which operate in those organisations. According to Paton (1994: 193):

> anyone who must regularly attempt to get things done with and through other people has the problem of generating agreement, or perhaps just consent, or at least compliance with regards to what must be done, how, when and on what terms. In doing that, those people will make use of whatever resources or means are available, and seem appropriate.

One of the most common resources used is power, and Paton describes four types of power:

- Position power

   This is the power which comes from a person's formal position in an organisation. The higher or more senior your position in an organisation, the more likely you are to exercise a greater degree of position power. Position power tends to attract status and respect, sometimes irrespective of how it is used. If you have position power in your organisation, you can generally use it in most situations, relative to that position in the organisation. The most obvious example of position power would tend to be the boss or head of any organisation.

- Expert power

   This is power which is more to do with specialist knowledge, skills and understanding than with position in an organisation, and indeed can be a power which at times exerts influence way above the position of the person who holds it in the organisation. Someone who is a technical expert with computers, for instance, could exercise a high degree of expert power even if they do not hold a senior position. When the head of the organisation's computer breaks down, the technicians hold considerable expert power. Expert power is likely to exert influence in fewer situations than position power.

- Dependence power

   This is power which relates to how much the different people in an organisation rely or depend on others in the organisation. If someone depends on you for something particular in the organisation, you have dependence power. There is some overlap with expert power, but a relatively low level of expertise can still exercise dependence power. If you are a group of people on whom others depend (such as the security staff who lock and unlock premises) you may be able to exercise power which is greater than position power. The difference is you will almost certainly be able to do this in only a limited number of situations.

- Personal power

   This is about 'those abilities and qualities which enable some people to make the most of whatever other power resources they have' (Paton 1994: 193). Charm, sensitivity, anticipation and self-confidence may all give you personal power. Depending on how well you are able to exercise this particular type of power, you may be able to insulate yourself reasonably well from any conflict resulting from other forms of power. We all know the people who appear to succeed whatever the circumstances. They have personal power.

These are not the only ways in which power operates, and you may at times feel you have none of those types of power. The key question to constantly ask is:

how can I use whatever combinations of power are available to the benefit of the students I am teaching?

Approaches to recognising and working with the power in your organisation are similar to those suggested in the chapter relating to managing conflict. Working through this thinking point will help you to more fully recognise the power relationships and responsibilities in your organisation.

Thinking point: who's got the power?

Look at the types of power described in this section and consider:

- Who has the different types of power in my organisation and how do they use it?
- What power do I have in the organisation and how do I use it?
- What power do I have with my students and how do I use it?

Strategy for survival: power to the people

There will be many times that power inside and outside your organisation will affect your working life, and by no means all will involve pain or disappointment. Power can be a positive and negative influence, and the trick is to be able to predict in advance the positive or the negative aspects of power in your organisation. The more difficult part is to then avoid the negative, or at least mitigate its effects, and ride the wave of the positive. Follow these golden rules, and they should help:

- Make sure you are aware of who has power in your organisation and why.
- Observe how that power is exercised, and how possible it may be to resist, counteract or avoid it.
- Be prepared with strategies to take advantage of opportunities which power may present.
- Do not use any power you may have to exploit others.
- You have more power than you may think with your students. Use it wisely.

References

Bate, P. (1994) Organizational culture. In Armson, R. and Paton, R. (eds) *Organisations: Cases, Issues, Concepts*. London: Paul Chapman Publishing.

Handy, C. (1995) *The Age of Unreason*. London: Arrow.

Paton, R. (1994) Power in organizations. In Armson, R. and Paton, R. (eds) *Organisations: Cases, Issues, Concepts*. London: Paul Chapman Publishing.

Senge, P. M. (1990) *The Fifth Discipline: The Art and Practice of the Learning Organization*. London: Random House.

Moving out of the deep end

17

Reality check

How's it going?

This chapter is aimed at providing you with a reality check for your teaching career to date, which we are confident will signal that you have now moved out of the 'deep end', and are growing in confidence that you will never return to its troubled waters. You will pause, reflect and ask yourself some crunch questions about how you feel, where you're going and where you plan to be in the next year or two. The chapter begins by offering you the chance to reflect on your teaching experiences to date, and how you have been managing them so far, using themes covered in earlier parts of the book. You will use these reflections to 'future gaze' about how your growing 'mastery' could enhance your career prospects in PCE, and what to consider when career opportunities arise. The chapter closes with a brief consideration of the idea of the *professional* in PCE, and the chance for you to ask yourself just how 'professional' you feel at this stage of your career.

Out of the deep end?

At the start of the book, we explained our goal as being 'to help you survive and develop as an effective, confident, committed and reflective teacher'. If you have been able to move some distance towards that goal, that is surely a cause for celebration. Although this book provides strategies to help you survive, you should by now have realised that developing your teaching to its full potential involves much more. What we also said right at the start of the book is that 'at some stage, and if you're both lucky and good at your job, you will often help to change someone else's world and life for the better'. It's a big job, isn't it? Just don't lose sight of this key message:

> being a teacher in PCE should be about more than 'just surviving'.

When a job has such elevated goals, regularly asking yourself 'how am I doing?' is not just sensible but essential. It can also help give you a sense of perspective, particularly if you share your thoughts with others who are ready to listen.

Checking back

A quick review of the chapter headings or thinking points in the book will remind you of the breadth and range of tasks, issues and activities a teacher in PCE is expected to cope with. However pressured and busy you have been, you will have regularly been reflecting on what has gone well, and what has not, as all teachers do. The chances are you will also have received considerable informal and formal feedback on your teaching and performance from others, as this is very much part of the scene in PCE. That feedback will probably have been based on standards, formal requirements or workplace expectations and may well have not covered what are some of the most important questions. Take some time out now to work through the 'deep end reality check', which we hope will raise useful questions, some of which have not yet been asked in this book.

Thinking point: deep end reality check

Working through the reality check as a task with other people will be helpful, although they will need to be those with whom you work closely. It can be a very effective team-building activity or peer review tool. With each question, ask yourself two things: 'How do I think I'm doing?' and 'How do others think I'm doing?' How you proceed is something you can decide for yourself, but you may wish to consider:

- grouping the statements and working on them over more than one session;
- putting your reflections on each statement down on paper (or word-processing them) as paragraphs, key words, mind maps, flow charts or images;
- rating each statement according to your degree of confidence in that area of your work, using 'very confident', 'confident', 'fairly confident' and 'lacking confidence';
- rating each answer numerically from high to low.

Reality check questions – ask yourself both of the questions below for each of the reality check bullet points which follow.

1 Do you think you are . . . ?
2 Do others think you are . . . ?

- Coping overall with the challenges of teaching in PCE
- Finding the positives in your work (is it rewarding, fun and enjoyable?)
- Feeling energetic, enthusiastic and resilient
- Changing lives and creating a civil society
- Riding the roller coaster of PCE through the wheel of learning

---

- Pushing the limits and being actively critical
- Developing your specialist subject and getting mentored
- Working effectively and inclusively with your students
- Keeping the 'learning' in 'e-learning'
- Managing conflict and dealing with paper, people and personal pressures
- Contributing to developing a learning organisation
- Understanding and working with power
- Enhancing your own and your students' appreciation of sustainability
- Developing the moral purpose of a teacher

Strategy for survival

Dealing with the types of problems which could occur from such a reality check is outside the scope of a book of this nature, but there are key pieces of advice we can give you:

- Make sure you do receive both 'official' and 'unofficial' supervision, mentoring and support within your working situation. Trying to solve problems and build on your strengths should not be your job alone.
- Use the confidence from areas you feel you do well in to build up your confidence in areas you feel less confident in. Look for improvement in small steps.
- Be ready to argue a calm and effective case when you need to, and stand your ground.

Prospects, possibilities and opportunities

Just how career prospects develop in PCE is less clearly defined than in other areas of education, and this is partly again because of the size, scope and diversity of the sector. When you are working in a large FE college with hundreds of staff, and you are on a permanent contract, teaching in a faculty team of 50, the routes you may take to development, promotion or advancement are reasonably clear (although not necessarily plentiful!). If you are working as a temporary part-time IT tutor in two learning centres, one in a company, and one in a neighbourhood adult education centre, on a one-year contract, where do you go from there? Many jobs are advertised and recruited through the conventional means, but many people progress in their careers as 'portfolio teachers', changing what they teach, where they work and who they work for on a regular basis, depending largely on supply and demand, or their own preferences. There are still large numbers of teachers who do not know if they are going to get paid work until literally their first session. If enough students arrive or register, the class goes ahead. If not there is no work. Many staff are also employed on short-term or agency contracts, because of funding associated with short-term initiatives and particularly in times of financial constraint. Providing advice on career prospects in PCE is therefore not exactly a precise science!

Often, if an opportunity arises, there is a momentum associated with it, which can make decisions rushed and ill thought through. At times things come along and you can't say no, or you aren't given the choice to say no. There is a saying 'decide in haste – repent at leisure' and it is particularly true here. We would argue that injecting thinking time into your career decisions is sensible, and here are some ways you can do that.

Thinking point: what, where and when?

First, you know best, or you should do, which parts of your work you enjoy most and least, and probably which parts of the job you excel at and are not so good at. You also know how much you need to earn to make ends meet. When you make decisions about your future, make sure you ask yourself these questions before deciding:

- *What* do I enjoy most about the job I do, *what* am I best at, and *what* do I really need to earn to survive?

- *Where* do I most enjoy doing the job, and feel most at home and at ease with my workmates and students?

- *When* might all of this change for the better or worse, and *when* should I do something about it?

Your answers can provide something of a 'health check' about your current situation, but should certainly mean you approach any choices you are presented with from a more informed perspective.

Taking opportunities

Because of the intense environment of change PCE operates within, a somewhat volatile and at times almost frighteningly unpredictable world is created. Carl Rogers's thoughts from 1983 seem just as relevant now as they were when he wrote them over 20 years ago:

> if there is one truth about modern man, it is that he lives in an environment that is *continually changing*.

> (Rogers 1983: 22)

Alongside ongoing and rapid change, opportunities can often be presented for those who are ready, willing and able to make the most of them. The difficulty with opportunity is that it often contains positive and negative components. If you say 'yes' to those extra paid teaching hours, will you still be able to prepare your teaching as fully as you do now? If you take on that coordinating role without any extra pay, is it really likely to lead to better-paid work in the future? In our experience, certain types of opportunities will probably arise when you are working in PCE. Is there such a thing as an opportunity you can't refuse? That's a difficult one to answer, but there are activities and opportunities which are genuinely useful, challenging and beneficial more often than they are not. Some of them can help to reawaken lost or hidden interests and abilities, and some can take you into new and exciting areas of experience and expertise.

Opportunities worth taking

Projects

Many projects each year contribute new developments, improvements and services, and most organisations in PCE get involved in them. They are often funded from sources outside the organisation, and include government initiatives, European-funded work, curriculum development and a large number of quality improvement activities. We would suggest you get involved in projects for a number of reasons:

- They give you a chance to operate and think somewhat 'outside the box' of the regular confines of your day-to-day schedule.
- You contribute to investigating and evaluating real activities and issues generally aimed at improving learning for your students.
- You will work with colleagues from other organisations or teams, and be able to 'showcase' your own work, and share effort across a wider community.
- You may get opportunities to travel locally, nationally or internationally as part of the work.
- You will be likely to develop new understandings and skills which will be directly helpful to you and your students.

Research

Some projects involve a research component, but research which is organised, structured and rigorous, and leads to outcomes such as published reports, is another positive opportunity. It can involve working in partnership with a recognised agency such as the Learning and Skills Research Network or a Centre for Excellence in Teacher Training, or arise as part of professional development or links with other organisations, universities or publishers. In addition to the advantages associated with projects, research can:

- lead to recognised publications in your field;
- develop deeper understandings of aspects of your own, and others', work;
- build your own profile in your field within and outside your organisation.

Creating

'Creating' is of course often involved in the best projects and research. What we are arguing, however, is that there is something special about the process of creating items as part of your work, using your own particular skills and experience, which needs to be preserved. This field of endeavour is often squeezed out of the normal range of day-to-day activity, but should not be. Creating can include developing learning materials and resources for your teaching; producing articles, web sites and blogs; scripting scenarios, plays, activities; building and making objects and artefacts. The particular benefits of creating are that it will:

- keep alive your own specialised skills and interests;
- enliven your 'normal' teaching work;
- reveal skills and understanding to others which they never knew you had;
- almost certainly enhance your students' learning.

Externalling

Perhaps more mundane, but equally important, externalling is about using your own particular expertise in a structured way to help others outside your immediate working situation to develop theirs. It can involve internal or external verification or moderation of learning programmes, working for quality assurance organisations, national awarding bodies and others, and its particular benefits include:

- using your own specialist expertise to help others improve their quality;
- comparing what you see externally with your own work and using it to enhance quality;
- contributing to the pool of expertise in your field;
- some of the work being paid.

To inject a final note of appropriate reality into this section, please remember this:

taking opportunities will always involve extra time and effort, but it is often worth it.

What is a professional?

By this stage of the book, the word 'professional' has been used on many occasions, and you will have your own understanding of what it means to be a professional in general terms, and in particular a 'professional teacher', or 'teaching professional'.

Thinking point: what do you think makes a 'professional teacher'?

If you were listing the qualities and characteristics of a 'professional teacher' in PCE, what would you come up with and why? Compare your results with at least one other person.

Professionalism in PCE

Randle and Brady (1997) presented a view of professionalism for PCE which included:

- the primary importance of student learning and the teaching process;
- maintaining loyalty to students and colleagues;
- expressing concerns for academic standards;
- recognition of teachers as experts;
- resources for education being made available on the basis of educational need;
- some elements of autonomy as essential;
- quality which is assessed on the basis of inputs and process;
- maintaining a spirit of collegiality.

For teachers this represents the combination of 'public sector values of service to the community, and a pedagogical concern for the individual learner' (Briggs 2005: 19)

The high degree of *individual and subject autonomy* represented in these views is difficult to maintain in the current environment of PCE, however, when external and internal controls are a powerful influence. The widespread use of institutional targets and performance measures, coupled with systems and procedures aiming to improve quality, leaves little space for the autonomous teacher.

Official statements about teaching professionals appear on the face of it to be encouraging, as in the recent workforce development plan for the FE workforce, which states:

> We need a Further Education Sector workforce which can support the creation of an inclusive society where all children and young people achieve their full potential and contribute to society and their communities.
>
> (Lifelong Learning UK 2007: 5)

Unfortunately, as is often the case, this positive message can get hidden amongst pages of turgid targets, actions and initiatives, or lost to practitioners in the field. When teachers in PCE are asked about their professional situation, a difficult and challenging version of reality tends to emerge. In a recent national FE staff survey, when asked for their views on the organisations they worked for:

People's views on their institutions are more worrying. Only 39.1% of staff say that they would recommend their organisation as a good place to work and this drops to 31.1% among lecturers and teachers. Furthermore, many respondents (42.2%) said that they don't feel valued by their employer.

(Learning and Skills Network 2008: 1)

Fortunately, the vast majority of teachers in the sector have a powerful commitment to the work they do with their students, despite the way they can be treated, and the same survey reported:

People believe that their job enables them to make a contribution to society, with 85.7% agreeing with this notion. This view is particularly strong among teaching staff (86.2%) and managers (88.2%). People also feel proud to work for the sector, with 74.4% reporting that this is the case.

(Learning and Skills Network 2008: 1)

It seems teachers in PCE do strongly consider themselves to be a group of people with a powerful and professional commitment to their students, even when working in an environment which doesn't support that very well. Wouldn't it be nice if that professionalism were recognised more often?

Pathway to a new professionalism?

Teaching is worth more than just delivering someone else's agenda, although it should always be accountable. We shall suggest in a later chapter that a real opportunity now exists to define the professional ground of a teacher in PCE, but we start here with some practical reflections on just where you may be on your professional journey so far.

Capable or extended professional?

Hoyle (1980) provides a useful view of professionalism for teachers, and describes two types of professionalism, which are at different ends of a continuum. He calls those at the two ends the 'restricted professional' and the 'extended professional', but, although using the idea of a continuum is useful, we prefer a different term. Given the range of pressures you work under in PCE, it's highly likely that you move between the 'extended' and 'restricted' mode at different times, and in different circumstances. The term 'restricted' downplays the essential and highly skilled roles of working hard and concentrating on your students. Isn't this in itself a highly positive achievement, especially early in your teaching career? We will use the term 'capable professional' as we believe it to be much more suitable.

- Capable professionals:
    - work hard, preparing their lessons and caring about their students;
    - limit their outlook, and do not think beyond their classroom or organisation;

- – do not consider the broader picture concerning the purposes of education as relevant to them;
- – are basically concerned with the practical and not with the wider theoretical aspects of their profession.
- ■ Extended professionals:
  - – seek to improve by learning from other teachers and professional development activities;
  - – constantly question and try to link theory to practice;
  - – are continually developing as teachers and placing their classroom work in a wider educational context.

Thinking point and strategy for survival: becoming an 'extended professional'

Consider where you feel you are currently as a professional.

- ■ Where between 'capable' and 'extended' would you see yourself most often?
- ■ What helps or hinders your progress towards the extended role?
- ■ What three steps can you take to move towards the extended side?
- ■ What help will you have available to do this from your organisation?

References

Briggs, A. (2005) Professionalism in Further Education: a changing concept. *Management in Education*, 19 (3): 19–23.

Hoyle, E. (1980) Professionalisation and deprofessionalisation in education. In Hoyle, E. and Megarry, J. (eds) *World Yearbook of Education, 1980: Professional Development of Teachers*. London: Kogan Page.

Learning and Skills Network (2008) *FE Colleges: The Frontline under Pressure? A Staff Satisfaction Survey of Further Education Colleges in England*. London: Learning and Skills Network.

Lifelong Learning UK (2007) *The Workforce Strategy for the Further Education Sector in England, 2007–2012*. Coventry: LLUK.

Randle, K. and Brady, N. (1997) Managerialism and professionalism in the 'Cinderella service'. *Journal of Vocational Education and Training*, 49 (1): 121–139.

Rogers, C. (1983) *Freedom to Learn in the 80s*. Columbus, OH: Charles Merrill.

18

Dealing with bureaucracy and inspection

This chapter begins with a reminder (as if you needed it!) of the scope of bureaucracy in PCE, and how at times it can seem to overwhelm the sector and all who work in it. Despite often genuinely highlighting and promoting good practice, inspection is one of the key creators of the PCE paper mountain, and we consider why that is the case. Using manuals and guidelines for inspectors and examples of organisations in PCE who have demonstrated excellence in teaching and learning, the chapter then provides the 'shining light or burning out' guide to making inspection work for you. We conclude this chapter by presenting our thoughts on other, more creative approaches to developing and ensuring quality in teaching and learning, with the 'people not paper manifesto'.

The ultimate paper pressure

'Paper pressure', as one of the three Ps of paper, people and personal pressure, has already briefly been mentioned in an earlier section. Although this chapter is in many ways about reducing paper pressure, and through it the other pressures, it would be a mistake to believe that teachers can manage without any bureaucracy or administration.

Inside every excellent teacher lives an excellent organiser and administrator.

Speed reading, summarising, planning and punctuality are just as important to the success of your teaching as imagination, inspiration and motivation. If you are assessing your students, you often need sophisticated skills of time management, judgement and clarity of explanation. Marking 30 assignments correctly and quickly enough to get them back to students in the time your student charter says you should is as much an achievement of organisation as of academic prowess. Necessary administration helping the wheel of learning to turn is one thing, but generating mountains of paper which bury it is another. To enrol a part-time student on a course lasting 20 hours, more than 10 documents often need to be completed. To provide evidence of the enrolment, initial assessment, progress, support, achievement and progression of one student can involve seven or eight different procedures, some of which are on paper, and some electronic. In the one 30-minute spell of struggling within a small piece of the maze of PCE bureaucracy, you could book a round-the-world trip, including stopovers, and eat a bar of chocolate! It must be possible to do things better.

Things can only get better

The purpose of inspection has been described as:

> to make judgements about the quality of education and training, the standards that are achieved by students, to evaluate the effectiveness of resources and their impact on learning.
>
> (Learning and Skills Development Agency 2004: 1)

This is reasonable enough, and remains current even though inspection frameworks have changed at least once since the statement was made. One of the key problems created, however, is the way in which inspection 'forces all practitioners to make *explicit* whatever may have been *implicit* before, i.e. if it cannot be seen it cannot be inspected' (Lea 2003: 77). A great deal of time is spent by a large number of teachers (and quality managers, administration staff and others) making sure that there is recognisable evidence of what we do, so that our peers, managers, inspectors and others are able to see it, and use it when judging us and our organisations, and comparing them with others. When inspectors have visited an organisation, one of the most frequent comments you hear from staff afterwards is 'I agree with what they said, and that's roughly what I would have expected.' At the extreme end of logic we could therefore argue that inspection can be an exercise in telling us what we already know. At the other end of the scale the obvious response would be: if an organisation already knew they had weaknesses in certain areas, why didn't they do something to change that before inspection? Perhaps a more telling question would be:

> How do we balance the time spent providing evidence of quality with the need to ensure we make time for improving quality?

Thinking point: prove it!

Reflect on your last week of work:

- What has worked really well, and why?
- What has not worked well, and why not?
- What difference has your teaching made to the learning of your students during the week?
- How do you know – what evidence do you have?
- How can that evidence help you make improvements?

Shining light or burning out?

Organisations which set the pace for PCE by achieving excellent results can be accorded 'beacon status', which 'celebrates learning providers that deliver outstanding teaching and learning' (LSIS 2009). Those who do not do so well tend to be 'named and shamed', then provided with help to improve, sometimes from the 'beacon' organisations. This culture of 'shining light' or 'burning out' is a tough one, so making the right choices about what you are doing regarding inspection is very important. Based on a number of publicly available documents and examples, here is our guide to help you and your organisation to be nearer to the 'shining light' than 'burning out'.

Quality assurance arrangements should:

- actively involve students and staff, and take account of what they say;
- be an integral part of day-to-day operations;
- show clearly how things do get better for students and staff;
- welcome suggestions for improvements to systems from staff and students;
- minimise the duplication of information and data and over-reliance on either paper or electronic forms;
- act as an early warning mechanism to detect problems and help to solve them;
- inform curriculum planning, initial teacher training and continuing professional development;
- celebrate and share good practice;
- produce an accurate picture of the 'state of play' in the organisation at that time.

If quality assurance in your organisation doesn't do these things, you need to do whatever you can to change it so that it does!

Strategy for survival: preparing for inspection

As an individual teacher preparing for inspection you need to:

- keep your course files (day-to-day teaching documentation) active, up to date and student-focussed;
- ensure that course reviews and evaluations are up to date, you have evidence of actions taken, and you can relate them to benchmark data;
- be able to track what has been happening on your courses for the last three years, including recruitment, retention and achievement;
- ensure you have organised any other relevant information about your teaching (such as course team minutes and external verifier reports), and that you can follow through actions you have taken at every stage.

Observation of teaching

Observation of teaching sessions has grown commonplace over the last five to ten years. As a new teacher you will almost certainly be observed on a number of occasions during your first year. You should also get the chance to observe others teaching. Being observed is a great opportunity to develop both your skills and understanding as a teacher, and the overall quality of teaching and learning in an organisation. The process of carrying out a teaching observation needs to be handled with considerable sensitivity, even if you are informally sitting in on a colleague's teaching, to get a feel for how they do it. We see teaching observation as a part of a learning process for teachers, and using it as a means of 'checking on' staff is to be avoided at all costs.

Observers of other teachers should:

- undertake training in lesson observation and feedback, which involves shadowing other observers;
- work to agreed approaches regarding criteria used; how and when feedback will be covered; judgements and grades used; and records completed.

When being observed you need to:

- plan the session to promote learning and attainment;
- demonstrate the capacity to differentiate tasks and activities to meet the needs of different students;
- demonstrate the ways you embed equality and diversity, language, literacy, numeracy and information technology in your teaching;
- monitor learning and participation for the duration of the session;
- provide students with detailed, constructive and evaluative feedback, which will help them progress;
- regularly self-evaluate sessions using a checklist, diary or other means.

Quality improvement which works

When organisations adopt the approaches this chapter has been advocating, it is possible to achieve genuinely good practice in developing, delivering and supporting learning. The following examples are all real examples from published accounts of inspection or best practice in PCE, which have been selected to represent best practice across the sector.

Local authority (LA) family learning programme

Family learning programmes are organised for parents and children to learn together, often to help families develop family literacy. This LA went through a series of stages when setting up its family learning programme, which helped to make sure it worked. Running throughout the programme is the involvement of all key people, effective communication, making changes based on feedback, and providing effective support for students and learning. By taking this approach it was possible to:

- agree which courses would be put on, based on detailed discussions with schools and families;

- run lively and engaging information and 'taster' sessions to include family suggestions for developing a suitable course;

- induct participants with maximum support and take account of different cultural and language needs;

- record learning and achievement on an ongoing and simple basis throughout the courses;

- provide opportunities for progression and achieving of qualifications.

Many of the students involved in this programme have grown considerably in confidence, gained recognised qualifications and progressed on to further learning.

Improving retention in hairdressing training

A large college operates hairdressing apprenticeships, which have recruited between 110 and 180 trainees each year over the last three years. Training takes place at the college, in the workplace and at outreach centres, and participants make some use of home study. The retention rate for these programmes has been low, on account of reduced trainee motivation caused primarily by a variety of factors including low wages, a sense of limited progress with the training, and few opportunities to make an impact in the workplace. A project team was set up to work with new apprentices, employers and the teachers involved, and first investigated more thoroughly the reasons for low retention, then strategies to change the situation. A wide range of employers, trainees and staff were involved, and the project:

- developed a more flexible approach to the training, with improved linkages between the workplace, the college and the staff involved;

- changed the curriculum to promote achievement at an early stage, and to add motivation for trainees;

- provided supportive trainee reviews more frequently, with regular employer involvement;

- used trainee, staff and employer feedback actively in developing the programme;

- actively celebrated success and publicised salon names.

The project contributed to a significant improvement in retention (31%) and committed and sustained support from employers for the approaches used. In addition, there have been a number of unexpected outcomes including stronger working relationships amongst all participants, smoother running of the college-based training and more use of support services by apprentices.

Teaching expert classes

Five further education colleges, two adult and community learning providers and two private training organisations gained some external funding from a Centre for Excellence in Teacher Training (CETT) for working together to develop an annual training day built around the idea of 'promoting excellence in teaching'. Teachers in those organisations who had an excellent teaching track record (as shown through observations, innovations or excellent achievement and retention) were approached as potential contributors. They were invited to a planning day to devise a mixture of sessions, or 'expert classes', around certain themes, and were given free reign on how to approach this within those themes. The resulting programme was made available to all teaching staff from all the organisations concerned, as an 'away day' at a centrally located conference venue. Facilitated discussion groups were interspersed with the expert classes, to provide a forum for issues raised. As the day progressed, 'scribes' within groups noted results, and these, participant evaluations and workshop presenter evaluations formed the basis of a report which was circulated to all attendees.

Results of the day showed that:

- The expert class leaders felt valued, enjoyed sharing their experiences, and identified areas where they could improve further.

- Participants in the day valued the workshops highly, but equally valued an opportunity to network and share views and experiences with others.

- The participating organisations noted increased confidence and motivation amongst their teaching teams, and a localised approach to developing expert classes.

- The event gained local, and in due course national, media coverage.

- Other areas that heard about the scheme planned to do something similar.

The people not paper manifesto

These examples in many ways illustrate what this closing section of the chapter is about to say, which is that

> bureaucracy and preparing for inspection doesn't have to be a painful drudge.

The focus throughout the examples above is on people, not on paper. The systems and processes are set up to draw people in, welcome their views and listen to what they say. This information is then compared with other relevant information, some of which is statistical and quantitative, and set in a wider context. Informed decisions on ways forward are made, action is taken, and the people are involved again in that action. Imagine this as an idealised (though possible) scenario for a 'people not paper' approach to quality assurance.

- You arrive at work, and log in to one of the staff computers. Three reminders pop up on your screen. Your second group of the day are due to complete their mid-course online evaluation questionnaire; at midday, you have a course team meeting, at which one of your colleagues is doing a mini-presentation on 'using tutorials to boost retention'; tomorrow is a 'feedback half day' which is reserved for all of the course advisory groups to take place across the organisation.

- After a tricky first session, for which three of your students were late, you log in to the agenda for the advisory group and put 'student lateness' on the agenda for the student reps to discuss.

- While your second group are completing their online questionnaire, and submitting the results to the centre for evaluation and development, you take a look at an analysis of the results from the last two years, provided by the centre, and update your own journal on actions taken. The system tells you your action plan has been updated, and your group returns for the face-to-face discussion of points they have raised, which is required at the mid-course evaluation stage.

- The presentation at your course team meeting provokes a lively discussion, and you go away thinking about trying out some of the things suggested. The course team secretary asks you to countersign the minutes, before they're added to the electronic course file.

- At the end of the day you stay for a few minutes to update your paper copy of your scheme of work to build in trying out the new ideas, and put it in the departmental admin pigeon hole, so that it can be updated tomorrow.

- You leave for home, tired, but upbeat, before 6 p.m.

References

Lea, J. (2003) Overview: the organization of post compulsory education. In Lea, J., Hayes, D., Armitage, A., Lomas, L. and Markless, S. (2003) *Working in Post-Compulsory Education.* Maidenhead: Open University Press.

Learning and Skills Development Agency (2004) *Quick Guide to Effective Practice: Inspections.* London: LSDA.

Learning and Skills Improvement Service (LSIS) (2009) *Learning and Skills Beacon Status* [Online] Excellence Gateway – Beacon Status [available at] http://beaconstatus.excellence.qia.org.uk/Index.html (accessed 15 December 2009).

19

Managing your managers

In an earlier chapter, when addressing the way power works in organisations, reference was made to 'position power' as 'the power which comes from a person's formal position in an organisation'. The people who hold most position power in organisations are usually (though not always) the managers. This chapter gets inside the nature and role of managers, starting with an explanation of the somewhat negative image of management in PCE. A glimpse into the manager's world follows, and an opportunity to recognise that they are also subject to many and varied pressures. We then reflect on the differences between managing and leading, and suggest there is perhaps too much of the first and not enough of the second in PCE. The chapter concludes with some hints and tips about how you can successfully work with and for your own managers as a teacher.

Management of PCE in context

The way management has developed in PCE over the last 20-plus years has been described as the 'new managerialism' (Randle and Brady 1997a; Lea 2003). Robson and Bailey (2009: 100), when discussing the current nature of the FE part of PCE, cite Nolan (2001) as follows:

> A further key feature is the importance of the manager's right to manage – leading to what is referred to as 'the new managerialism', with its focus on change management rather than system maintenance and the stress on outputs rather than procedures.

To put it simply, 'managerialism' is a term which is used to describe the use of business approaches, systems and practices in the public sector which were originally more commonplace in the private sector. Managerialism emphasises two key areas, accountability and efficiency, and normally involves:

- ensuring recruitment, retention and achievement of students are paramount;
- balancing efficiency and effectiveness;
- focussing key activity on the organisation, rather than the individuals within it;

- flexibility of teaching staff within the needs of the organisation;

- organising the resources for education on the basis of market demand and value for money;

- basing quality assurance on outputs and performance indicators;

- placing control of the organisation and its activities in the hands of the managers (adapted from Randle and Brady 1997b).

A number of influential writers have argued that new managerialism and the changes in the PCE environment have brought with them negative consequences for teachers, students and organisations including:

- a reduction in the level of consultation with staff, and the concentration of power at the centre of an organisation in the hands of a few;

- an emphasis on enterprise, income generation, local competition and survival in the marketplace at the expense of more general educational goals;

- an intensification of work through increased hours of teaching, and greater accountability to, and closer supervision, by their line managers;

- the loss of influence or autonomy in teachers' working lives, as they feel that their self-management is replaced by managerial command and control (Avis 1996; Ainley and Bailey 1997; Lomas 2003; Robson 2006; Watson and Crossley 2001).

Overall, one would have to say that, sadly, many people working in PCE will experience this type of management on occasions, if not on a regular basis. How then do we work within that as teachers? First let's give some further attention to who the managers may be.

Who are the managers?

Once again, the diversity of PCE presents us with a problem. In a small organisation, everyone may to some degree have a management responsibility. Even in a large FE college, many roles involve taking responsibility in a management sense. A section head in a large college may manage a greater budget than the whole of an Adult and Community Education department at a local authority. Common management roles which do exist in PCE are:

- *principal* – the most commonly used name for the head of a further education college (and at times other PCE organisations);

- *senior manager* – usually part of a small group who make up the executive management of any organisation, such as directors or finance managers;

- *head of department/faculty* – person with overall responsibility for a curriculum area, or group of related curriculum areas such as health and social care, humanities, construction;

- *cross-institutional manager* – one who works across an organisation with a developmental, service or organisational role such as head of learning support, management information services, quality management, learning resources;
- *middle manager* – not part of the senior management team, but undertaking management responsibilities.

Even within these roles, there can often be blurring of the boundaries between them, depending on the size and nature of the organisation. One key factor, which we are not necessarily presenting as negative, but which certainly has a major impact, is this:

> many senior managers in PCE may not come from an educational background, and may never have taught at all.

Thinking point: who are your managers?

- Who manages your organisation, and what effect does that have on you and your students?
- How are decisions made, and do you have any influence?

What does a manager in PCE do?

The following two examples of managers are deliberately from different PCE contexts to illustrate the varied demands of day-to-day management. Although very different in many ways, both managers also encounter a surprisingly similar range of challenges.

The company learning centre manager

Michael manages a learning centre in a company with 230 employees. The centre has an open access computer suite, an office and two classrooms/seminar rooms. There is also a small library with books, journals, resources and access to online collections. In addition to being the learning centre manager, Michael is the union learning champion in the company, and manages access to the centre by the local community and local businesses, which is a requirement of the funding which set up the centre. An inspection of the local learning centres is taking place in three months, and the self-assessment plan for that visit is due in very soon. The three paid staff of the centre are coming to the end of their one-year contracts, and at least one will be losing their job unless the centre gets nearer to hitting its annual targets. A major bid for new funding for the next three years, which Michael is writing, is due in next week. The next basic IT course, which Michael is teaching, starts in 10 minutes and two of the computers are down. Employees working shifts have been complaining they can't get access to the centre immediately before or after the night shift.

The college principal

Aminah has been in her job for three weeks, and has taken over a college with mediocre inspection results. Improving that situation is one of her key responsibilities. The proposed budget for the next financial year is showing a need for efficiency gains, which will leave little scope for improving the ageing buildings or the college campuses. A new government policy requires all new teaching staff to take an introductory 'survival course' to make sure they can start teaching effectively as quickly as possible, and the teacher trainer who would be teaching this course has just gone off on long-term sickness leave. At her most recent senior management meeting Aminah was relieved to get a positive response from the rest of the executive to her proposals for the future of the college, though the head of curriculum explained that the staffing cuts 'could be tricky', especially with respect to discussions with the union and academic committee involved. Aminah has just heard that her offer on a local house has been accepted, so she will shortly be able to move out of the hotel she has been living in for the past month.

Thinking point: do you want to be a manager?

We have of course exaggerated to some degree to illustrate the point, but these are genuine problems and dilemmas which our managers in PCE face every day.

- How would you respond to the challenges in these examples?
- Could you balance educational and management values to make decisions?
- Would you need to compromise your own views and values, and how would that make you feel?
- Would you rather leave management to someone else?

Management or leadership?

As you can see from the examples given, much of what managers face involves what is immediate or impending. Management is more than 'fire fighting' and working with the 'here and now', but at times it can be difficult to move outside the short term. Examining some of the potential differences between 'managing' and 'leading' helps to understand some of the pressures, and to find ways forward. McGrath (2004) produces a useful analysis of 'what managers are concerned with', and 'what leaders are concerned with', drawing on a number of other sources in the field (Table 19.1).

We are not arguing for either a 'management only' or a 'leadership only' approach. As Glatter (1997: 188) nicely puts it, 'indifferent management can be good enough to secure survival in some contexts, while even talented leadership can fail to prevent closure or amalgamation in others'. A later chapter concentrates more on leadership, but we would argue that the key is to be balanced:

a blend of management and leadership should be the goal for PCE.

TABLE 19.1 Managers and leaders

MANAGERS ARE CONCERNED WITH	LEADERS ARE CONCERNED WITH
The present	The future
Planning and budgeting	Building vision and developing strategy
Monitoring and control	Exercising influence
Providing a sense of order, staying on the right path and doing things right	Providing a sense of purpose and doing the right things
Maintenance of systems and the status quo	Working positively with change
Organisational structure and staffing	Drawing people together and building consensus
Problem solving	Problem seeking
Economy and efficiency	Effectiveness
Staying on course	Making new paths

Adapted from McGrath (2004).

Leading from the middle

How can that blend and balance be best achieved? In her analysis of FE middle managers' roles in strategic decision making, Leader (2004) suggests that

managers can lead from the middle.

This statement is used in relation to middle managers, but is very much about balancing managing and leading. Management in PCE would benefit by moving away from overconcentration on managing day to day and towards leading the sector to a more positive future. In simple terms, this is about moving away from management towards leadership. If these key principles were adopted, it could make a significant difference:

- Never lose sight of the key mission of providing inclusive learning opportunities for your students.
- Day-to-day business is important, but there is a tomorrow.
- Inclusive approaches to managing will work.
- Trust the autonomy and capability of middle managers and teachers.
- Devolve leadership.
- A practical, systematic approach to organisation and communication is appreciated by staff.
- A shared vision may be better than your vision.
- You are allowed to be nice and still be a manager.

Managing your managers

This is essentially your strategy for survival in this area. First, don't forget what we have already said repeatedly about the ways you work with your students and your colleagues. You may find it more difficult to be 'actively critical' with your managers, but what you have learnt about group dynamics, personality types and organisations is essential to understand and manage your own managers (and for you to use if you become a manager!). Follow these guidelines, adapted from Geisler (1999), and you should work well with your managers:

- Know your manager's style.

  How does he or she prefer to interact with staff? Face-to-face meetings? Memos? Email? Drop-in visits, or by appointment? Is there any social communication, or is it all business?

- Be sensitive to your manager's current challenges.

  The more you know about your manager's current workload, the better you can work out how and when to add to (or reduce) that workload. This is largely a matter of being aware of what is going on in your organisation, but is also about the bigger picture, and simple observation.

- Timing is important.

  Be aware that some times are better than others to approach (or disagree with) your manager, and be able to 'pick your moments'.

- Know your manager's values.

  If you can (and wish to) connect with your manager's values, this could increase the prospects of the manager being on your side. Be prepared for clashes of values, and think carefully about how to work with that. Negotiation is almost always more effective than confrontation.

- Communicate positively.

  Don't forget what we have described in a previous chapter as 'active calmness . . . which is a combination of relaxed self-awareness and positive thinking.' Be prepared to have ideas and actions challenged, and think through how to respond to that challenge in advance.

- Follow up and follow through.

  Don't forget that you are by no means all that a manager has to deal with. If you need to remind them, provide more information, or indeed give support in any way, make sure you do.

  Now be brave and try it out!

References

Ainley, P. and Bailey, B. (1997) *The Business of Learning*. London: Cassell.

Avis, J. (1996) The enemy within: quality and managerialism in education. In Avis, J., Bloomer, M., Esland, G., Gleeson D. and Hodkinson, P. (eds) *Knowledge and Nationhood*. London: Cassell.

Geisler, J. (1999) *Managing Your Manager: Addressing Your Important Issues*. St Petersburg, FL: Poynter Institute.

Glatter, R. (1997) Context and capability in educational management. *Educational Management & Administration*, 25 (2): 181–192.

Lea, J. (2003) Overview: the organization of post compulsory education. In Lea, J., Hayes, D., Armitage, A., Lomas, L. and Markless, S. (2003) *Working in Post-Compulsory Education*. Maidenhead: Open University Press.

Leader, G. (2004) Further education middle managers: their contribution to the strategic decision-making process. *Educational Management Administration & Leadership*, 32 (1): 67–79.

Lomas, L. (2003) Accountability and effectiveness in post-compulsory education. In Lea, J., Hayes, D., Armitage, A., Lomas, L. and Markless, S. (2003) *Working in Post-Compulsory Education*. Maidenhead: Open University Press.

McGrath, J. (2004) Management and leadership in post-compulsory education. In Coles, A. (ed.) *Teaching in Post-Compulsory Education: Policy, Practice and Values*. London: David Fulton Publishers.

Nolan, B. C. (ed.) (2001) *Public Sector Reform: An International Perspective*. Basingstoke: Palgrave.

Randle, K. and Brady, N. (1997a) Further education and the new managerialism. *Journal of Further and Higher Education*, 21 (2): 229–239.

Randle, K. and Brady, N. (1997b) Managerialism and professionalism in the 'Cinderella service'. *Journal of Vocational Education and Training*, 49 (1): 121–139.

Robson, J. (2006) *Teacher Professionalism in Further and Higher Education: Challenges to Culture and Practice*. London: Routledge.

Robson, J. and Bailey, B. (2009) Bowing from the heart: an investigation into discourses of professionalism and the work of caring for students in further education. *British Educational Research Journal*, 35 (1): 99–117.

Watson, G. and Crossley, M. (2001) Beyond the rational: the strategic management process, cultural change and post-incorporation further education. *Educational Management and Administration*, 29 (1): 113–125.

VI

Moving towards mastery

20

If only . . .

This chapter sets the scene for the final section of the book by taking stock of where PCE as a sector appears to be positioned as we start the second decade of the twenty-first century. A discussion of the distance which has developed between the ideas and practices of teaching and learning and the approaches of government is followed by a consideration of the most powerful themes and issues which seem likely to steer the sector and the work of teachers in PCE for the next several years, namely economic recovery, employer engagement, customer care and workforce development. We close the chapter with a reminder of what we believe teachers could claim as their priorities for the future rather than have others set the agenda for them.

THE DISTANCE BETWEEN US

The situation of the sector at present, as we have established in earlier chapters, is one in which teachers are powerfully committed to supporting their students and to helping them achieve, placing teaching and learning at the heart of what they do, and often achieving excellent results. In contrast to this, government and associated agencies and organisations appear to become more distant and directive, and at times appear to forget teaching and learning almost completely. A powerful recent publication by Frank Coffield argues this case forcefully:

> In an age of government priorities and targets, teaching and learning remain close to the hearts of many post-16 education professionals.
>
> (Coffield 2008: foreword)

> We are all familiar with current practice: ritual genuflection is made to the central importance of learning, but the sermon swiftly becomes a litany of what the government considers to be the really key elements of transformation – priorities, targets, inspection grades and funding – and the topics of teaching and learning disappear from sight, as if they had no momentum or dynamic of their own.
>
> (Coffield 2008: 1)

A growing distance between teachers and other professionals and politicians, policy makers and the associated organisations has developed in recent years, and teachers generally feel as if they are being 'done to', rather than 'worked with'. Fortunately, and somewhat amazingly, this hasn't stopped them from working extremely hard to help their students achieve. It has often, however, made what is a demanding profession more difficult than it needs to be. Coffield suggests there is a way out of this situation:

> Staff need to be involved as full, equal partners in the development, enactment, evaluation and redesign of policy, because tutors and managers are the people who turn paper policies into courses, curricula and purposeful activities in classrooms.
>
> (Coffield 2008: 22)

Just how much of a willingness really exists to allow teachers into that process remains to be seen.

The current agenda in PCE

At the time of writing this edition, the world is in the grip of a major global recession, which has already impacted on teachers, learners and whole communities, and will continue to do so for some years. Post-compulsory education will play an extremely important role in helping us emerge from the recession, and the economic situation has reinforced the steer from government in four key areas: economic recovery; employer engagement; customer care; and workforce development.

Economic recovery and employer engagement

A recent 'skills strategy' document from the government sets the scene succinctly:

> Increasing our skills base is critical to the recovery and the long term success of the UK economy.
>
> (BIS 2009: 2)

In the same document, the approach to involving employers and businesses, or 'employer engagement' as it is often called, is also spelt out:

> Key to both the relevance of the skills we fund and the ability of learners to dictate priorities are the needs and expectations of business and industry. Our expectations of business are going to rise sharply: they need to be collaborating with colleges and training institutions (including the Third Sector) to create courses that meet their needs; communicating those needs better to students; and valuing investment in their workforce. Because they will be the key beneficiaries of a more vocational, more demand-led system, businesses will also be expected to contribute more to the costs of a world-class system.
>
> (BIS 2009: 3)

Teachers and organisations across PCE have been engaged with employers for as long as there have been employers, and the work done in this area is often unrecognised, but the degree to which individual teachers are likely to become involved in work with employers and outside their own organisations has been rising and will probably continue to do so. Working outside your own classroom, visiting employers, training employees and involving employers both in the classroom or learning site and in the development of curriculum is already becoming a regular part of the work of many teachers in PCE.

Customer care

Most people will have a working understanding of what 'customer care' is and what it involves, and will have experienced different levels of it in their local high street. What a teacher might ask is 'why are we talking about customer care when we are working with students, not customers?' The Macmillan Online Dictionary offers us this definition of customer care:

> the activity of looking after customers, and helping them with any complaints or problems.
>
> (Macmillan 2010)

Although this may seem a little alien to education, it is not unreasonable to expect us to look after our students and help them with complaints and problems, and we are surely doing that as teachers every day. Many of our students or their employers have directly paid for their courses through fees, or through their taxes, so in that sense they are also customers, and will increasingly expect good customer care from us. We would like to venture a broader definition of customer care as it operates for teachers:

> Customer care is the process by which we help our students, their organisations or employers and their communities to develop and extend their capability, confidence and achievement to such a degree that they will come back to us for more.

Workforce development

Post-compulsory education has also long been involved in workforce development of one sort or another, whether through running courses for employers, preparing young adults for employment, or training those who train employees. In the context of this book, however, we are considering the development of the workforce in PCE, as this has assumed a growing importance over the last eight to ten years, since training to teach in PCE became mandatory. The current goals of workforce development are summarised in the sector document as follows:

> It is vital for us all in England to ensure that the entire further education workforce is appropriately trained, has the flexibility to respond to these changing needs and is recruiting the best people from a wide talent pool.
>
> (LLUK 2009: 1)

In case you are not sure, what is called 'the further education sector' in the quote from LLUK is what we are calling PCE. So what difference will this emphasis on workforce development make to teachers in the sector? One thing you can be sure of is that there will continue to be opportunities for you to develop your practice as teachers, through structured training, CPD and other learning opportunities. This is a good thing and we have argued throughout the book that a teacher who is interested in developing is likely to be a better teacher. What unfortunately may take all of your survival skills and experience as a teacher, and as a human being, is working out just how you will fit this all in alongside everything else we have introduced in the book, and caring for your student and engaging with employers, especially when you may well not get any additional time to do it!

Thinking point: employer engagement and customer care in action

This thinking point is based on a real example. A new principal was brought in to revive the fortunes of a college which had failed its inspection. The college started by finding out what employers thought of it, and discovered they had a reputation for poor communication and a lack of consultation, that they didn't offer the training employers wanted, and that the quality of the training which was offered was not felt to be good. The college used a recognised framework of national standards to help it develop and improve its engagement with sectors and individual employers. A detailed action plan was produced that made it clear to all why the college was not effectively engaging with employers and what was going to be done to put it right. Real efforts were made to become customer focused in all areas, including at course level, and this was supported by monthly visits by the head of workforce development to all heads of department to discuss progress on agreed targets. In a more recent assessment of their employer engagement they were found to have improved and grown spectacularly.

How does this compare with your organisation?

Strategy for survival: getting engaged

A recently produced 'quick start guide' to working with employers (Quality Improvement Agency 2008) contains some useful hints and tips, and these are included as part of this strategy for survival.

Ways of working with a local business

Working with a local business can take many forms, all of which have value. The term 'local business' can include public sector organisations and voluntary groups, as well as private businesses.

Try the following approaches:

- *Fact-finding missions* – learners visit a local business to research a specific topic, such as how the business uses IT to manage the supply chain.

- *Hot seat* – a representative of a local business comes to your premises and answers questions posed by the learners. The visitor is invited to take the 'hot seat', hence the title of the activity. The rules are simple: the learners can ask any question they like, but the person in the hot seat can refuse to answer the question.

- *Employer challenge* – a local business sets a challenge for learners, based on a real problem that it is trying to solve. Learners' proposed solutions are judged by someone from the business. Learners may even help the business to implement the solution.

- *Enterprise project* – learners set up and run their own IT-related business. There are a number of national bodies and initiatives that can help with this, such as Young Enterprise and The Prince's Trust.

Getting engaged

How engaged with employers do you feel you and your organisation are? Try one of the activities above and see how it works.

Sustainable development in education

We have given key 'themes from outside' (i.e. those which are being steered by people who are not teachers) a reasonable airing during the chapter to date, so we will now conclude with two key issues for the future which come 'from inside' (i.e. our own views and values as teachers).

> Our biggest challenge this new century is to take an idea that seems abstract – sustainable development – and turn it into a reality for all the world's people.
>
> (Kofi Annan, Former UN Secretary General, 2001)

This is one of the most used quotes you will come across if you search for content on sustainability, but sums up the situation really well, and highlights a crucial issue for PCE, which is:

> How can we as teachers help sustain the planet as we know it?

This does sound melodramatic but, as an extremely useful recent publication on sustainable development in the curriculum puts it:

> The challenge of sustainability is one for us and for the communities we live in. Yet it is a unique challenge because as learning providers we are the issue and the

opportunity, the problem and the solution. To make a positive impact, sustainability needs to resonate with people in their daily lives.

(SORTED 2009: 4)

Clearly we can't get very far with this in one part of one chapter in one book, but there is some key advice all teachers can attend to, and we will attempt to introduce it here.

Thinking point: embedding sustainable development

Answering these questions should help move you on as a teacher in this area.

- Just how much do you already know about sustainable development in education, and where can you find out more?
- What do you know abut your organisation's policy and practice relating to sustainability?
- What efforts have you made to find out who else in your organisation or from outside may be able to help you with sustainable development?

Strategy for survival: what can I do straight away?

- Search the Internet for 'sustainability' or 'education for sustainable development'. There is a growing amount of good material out there.
- *What you can do today* is introduce a 10- or 20-minute 'podule' on some aspect of sustainable development into a teaching session.
- *What you can within a week or two* is make minor modifications to your teaching within your existing curriculum.
- *What you can do in a few months* is revise existing schemes of work and lesson plans to take account of sustainability.
- Share what you come across and use with at least one other colleague.

Sustaining teaching and learning in PCE

We have made many comments about the dedication of teachers and the effect this has on students throughout the book, and have regularly contrasted this with the way in which the sector is governed, regulated and managed. Just how then can the gap between the reality for the teacher and the rhetoric of the government be reduced? What is it that we are promoting? Overall it is the nature of teaching as part of a valued, important and transforming process of education. Frank Coffield (2008) again sums this up beautifully.

something vital to the whole enterprise is being forgotten. I learned from my father, as he learned from his, to hear the music, the excitement and the hope in the word 'education'. I also learned that it is the job of teachers to help other people's children to hear and respond to that music. We do it because teaching is a noble profession, which dedicates itself to the lot of those who have not had our advantages. We do it because we believe in social justice and, like our parents and grandparents, we want a better world for ourselves, our children and all children. That is the meaning of our lives as teachers.

(Coffield 2008: 61)

We believe that changing things often takes a long time, and what is important is that people know they are, first, trying to help change take place and, second, feeling that some progress is being made. Small steps can make a big difference, especially if many people make those small steps together! Here therefore are some small steps we can all take.

Strategy for survival: one small step

- Note down two clear examples of learning you have seen happen during the week and the effect that they had on your students.
- Select one learning activity you really think works well and persuade one other teacher to try it out.
- Tell your line manager about two examples of good teaching you have experienced this week.
- Organise a mini learning party for your students to celebrate their success.
- Organise a similar mini celebration for at least two colleagues to join where you can all celebrate together.

The remaining chapters of this book are intended to help you move further out of the deep end and into a position where you can be part of trying to return teaching and learning to the heart of what we do as teachers.

References

Annan, K. (2001). *Sustainable Development: Humanity's Biggest Challenge in the New Century*. Speech given in Bangladesh, March 2001. [Online. Available at] http://www.unis.univienna.org/unis/pressrels/2001/sgsm7739.html (accessed 1 June 2010).

BIS (2009) *Strategy Document: Skills Investment Strategy 2010–11*. London: Department of Business, Innovation and Skills.

Coffield, F. (2008) *Just Suppose Teaching and Learning Became the First Priority*. London: Learning and Skills Network.

LLUK (2009) *The Workforce Strategy for the Further Education Sector in England, 2007–2012 – Revised version: 2009–2010*. London: LLUK.

Macmillan (2010) [Online] Macmillan Online Dictionary [available at] http://www.macmillandictionary.com/dictionary/british/customer-care (accessed 20 January 2010).

Quality Improvement Agency (2008) *Working with Employers: A Quick Start Guide to Engaging with Local Businesses*. London: QIA.

SORTED (2009) *Creating the Conditions for Embedding Sustainable Development in the Curriculum*. Cheltenham: Sustainability Online Resources Toolkit for Education.

21

Developing leadership skills

In the last chapter of Part V we considered some general aspects of management and leadership, and a number of strategies and principles you could use to understand and manage your manager. This chapter begins with a more detailed consideration of different types of leadership in PCE, introducing four models which are relevant. It continues by providing the 'take me to your leader checklist' for you to assess your leadership capability across the four key areas of leading yourself, leading your students, leading other people and leading across organisations. The chapter closes with examples of successful leadership in PCE by showcasing management which has been effective in the real world.

Leadership in PCE today

An image of somewhat negative leadership styles across the sector tends to emerge from research. This comment on FE colleges is reasonably typical:

> For FE teachers, the experience of working in the corporate college has been represented as the intensification of work through increased hours of teaching, and greater accountability to, and closer supervision by, their line managers. Consequently, they often report the loss of influence or autonomy in their working lives, as they feel that their self-management is replaced by managerial command and control.
>
> (Robson and Bailey 2009: 101)

We believe we all have a responsibility to try to change that situation, so are taking a positive stance to what leadership can be in this chapter. After all you may be a future leader, so why not start developing your approach early?

There are four types of leadership which are particularly relevant to PCE. They have been defined as follows:

Transactional leadership

Transactional leadership is based upon legitimate authority or positional power within an organisational structure. The emphasis is on the clarification of goals and objectives, work tasks and outcomes, organisational rewards and punishments. Transactional leadership requires mutually dependent interpersonal interactions between leaders and members.

(Learning and Skills Development Agency 2003: 5)

This is a leadership style whereby your leaders need you to carry out defined tasks and goals. If the outcomes of those tasks and goals meet what the leadership needs, you are likely to get a reward. If not, you are likely to be punished. The rewards are expected to provide motivation, and the punishment a means of correcting incorrect behaviour. Power within the organisation is concentrated in the hands of a small number of people.

Transformational leadership

Transformational leadership engenders high levels of motivation and commitment among followers/members. The emphasis is on generating a vision for the organisation and the abilities of leaders to appeal to the 'higher' ideals and values of followers/members in order to achieve high performance, high commitment and high inclusion to an organisation or system. Often associated with charismatic leadership and with organisational change, this form of leadership 'transforms' employees to pursue organisational goals over self-interest.

(Learning and Skills Development Agency 2003: 6)

This is a leadership style whereby you are motivated to work for the benefit of the organisation and its students, rather than for yourself, and goals and efforts are shared across the whole staff team. Rewards are associated with achieving successful transformation and being a positive part of that change. Power within the organisation is still concentrated within a small group of people, and often in the hands of a charismatic leader.

Synergistic leadership

Much theory about leadership, even when it is promoting a democratic approach, has failed 'to include concerns of diversity and (the) female voice' (Learning and Skills Development Agency 2003: 7). **Synergistic leadership** is seen as a way of taking more account of diversity issues and the female voice. The role of a synergistic leader shifts from exercising power or inspiring transformation to creating an environment where the full diversity of a workforce is taken account of, and the building blocks put in place to make full use of that diversity for the benefit of all concerned.

This leadership style recognises and values expertise, not rank or position, and aims to put everyone in the workforce on an equal footing. Professional development is highly valued, and an atmosphere of nurturing and caring is present. Motivation is generated through an emphasis on both individual value and contribution to the organisation-wide community of practice. Leadership does still tend to be the province of a small group of people.

Distributed leadership

> **Distributed leadership** theory casts leadership beyond individual agency to show how leadership practice is a social process concerned with leadership thinking and action in situ. It focuses on how leadership is distributed . . . concentrating on leadership activity rather than role or position, and on how leadership is stretched over people and situations rather than the individuals' leadership traits.
>
> (Learning and Skills Development Agency 2003: 7)

This leadership style sees the organisation as a web of interconnected processes, people and situations, which all combine to achieve its goals. Specialised expertise is recognised and individuals and groups are given responsibility to solve problems and share ideas and efforts. Leadership is seen as everyone's responsibility, and the leadership structure is developed to support and sustain that collective motivation. Everyone has leadership responsibility and the group of senior leaders must facilitate the effective carrying of that responsibility.

Thinking point: transaction, transformation, synergy or distribution?

Reflect on your own experiences of leading and being led.

- Which of the four leadership styles have you experienced?
- How has that leadership affected you and the work you were doing?
- How did it affect others such as students, colleagues, friends and family?
- What leadership style do you prefer and why?

Does leadership affect performance?

There is some evidence to suggest leadership can transform organisations, and impact on learner outcomes, although little of this evidence comes from PCE. Robinson *et al.* (2008) examined a variety of 'leadership interventions' in 27 studies which had evaluated the ways in which leadership could impact on learner outcomes in schools, and did find that leadership could make a real difference. Four different 'dimensions' of impact were described in the article, and interestingly the one which appeared to have most impact on results was that described as the 'promoting and participating in teacher learning and development' dimension (Robinson *et al.* 2008). This highlights something which points to an essential and often underestimated aspect of PCE and other public sector organisations. When you are the teacher or one of the other staff working directly with students it is fairly self-evident, but it is surprising how often it is not recognised by the leaders in an organisation. When we consider the degree to which power in many of the leadership models is concentrated in the hands of a few, and the pressures on the leaders themselves to comply in many ways, perhaps it is not surprising. Our central message in terms of leadership is very clear:

> Those who make the most difference to the students are their teachers,
> their fellow students and their closest friends and family.

Any approach to leadership which does not recognise, support, develop and make positive use of that capacity of the teachers to make a difference is misguided.

Take me to your leader

Distributed leadership and *synergistic leadership* are both attracting considerable interest at present. They both recognise shared responsibility, problem-solving approaches and individual and team expertise, and emphasise the importance in any public service of the front-line workers. In simple terms, if your teachers are working at full effectiveness with their students in a consistent manner across the organisation, the chances are everyone will be more satisfied and achievement will improve. For this to work, and for more people in your teams to develop leadership capability, time and resources need to be invested in *leadership development*.

Leadership development activities

Don't worry, we are not suggesting you go off to the jungle and build huts or wrestle with giant insects, much as you may want to! These 'take me to your leader' activities are intended to let you think about the leader in you, through the use of a self-rating checklist, and a group exercise. They reflect a combination of accepted positive leadership models, and our own vision of the 'reflective professional', which is central to the next chapter. The four key areas of leadership are:

- *Leading yourself* – this is about the ways in which you understand and work with your own strengths and weaknesses; how effectively you communicate overall; how ready you are to take responsibility for your own actions; what your approaches are to risk taking, innovation and change; and your capacity to plan for the future and develop your capabilities.

- *Leading your students* – this is about the way you understand, work and communicate with your students; how you develop their capacity to take responsibility for their own actions; how you encourage them to innovate, take risks and manage change; and how you assist the development of their capacity to plan and develop towards the future.

- *Leading other people* – this is about how you understand, work and communicate with other people at all levels of your organisation; how you help them to develop their capacity to take responsibility for their own actions; how you work collaboratively with them to innovate, take risks and manage change; and how you work with others towards the development of their capacity to plan and develop towards their own future goals and those of the organisation.

■ *Leading across organisations* – this is about how you can work and communicate across institutional boundaries at all levels; how you contribute to developing a responsible and accountable organisation; how you foster balanced risk taking, innovation and change management; and how you create conditions for a forward-looking and responsive organisation to thrive.

Thinking point: take me to your leader self-assessment (Table 21.1)

When completing the checklist give yourself an honest rating for each question from 1 to 4. If you feel the answer is different for different situations, complete more than one checklist. The key to the rating is:

1 = no competence;

2 = some competence but need more development;

3 = generally competent in most situations;

4 = competent in all but a few situations.

Once you have scored yourself, interpreting the results is easy. There are 30 questions in all, making a maximum rating of 120 and a minimum of 30. Overall scores could be interpreted as follows:

0–30	You either misunderstood the questions or need to build your confidence and experience across most areas.
30–70	You are showing some leadership potential, and need to develop an action plan based on improving your weakest areas.
70–90	You have sound leadership capability and can plan ahead with some confidence to build further on these results.
90–120	You can feel very pleased at your leadership rating, but don't get complacent, as PCE changes very fast!

Whatever your results, think them through and make plans to improve on the areas you didn't score so well on, and reinforce the ones you did.

Leadership in the real world

These two examples illustrate positive leadership across a community-based adult learning organisation, and within a small teaching team.

Adult learning centre

A large rural county provides an adult education service operating through a network of local centres, each with considerable autonomy. The range of courses is very wide,

TABLE 21.1 Take me to your leader self-assessment

NO.	AREA	RATING			
		1	2	3	4

Gaining respect of your students, work colleagues, managers and others

1	Being familiar with the educational and professional backgrounds of your students and colleagues
2	Listening actively, consulting widely and being open to the concerns of others
3	Building shared views and goals
4	Treating all others with respect and fairness
5	Working collaboratively to solve problems
6	Encouraging thinking 'outside the box'
7	Arguing positive cases effectively with senior managers and peers

Developing individuals and groups through direct and indirect day-to-day interactions

8	Developing learning, work and organisational objectives as a shared enterprise
9	Promoting innovative and creative approaches
10	Negotiating access to appropriate people, physical and financial resources to achieve objectives
11	Agreeing and carrying out strategies to monitor and review achievement of the objectives, and developing appropriate evaluation tools
12	Working towards the planned objectives in an organised manner
13	Agreeing and making necessary changes to objectives as needed
14	Building individual and group ownership of the objectives

Energising performance – supporting others in working to effectively fulfil their potential, and complete activities

15	Maintaining clear and positive channels of communication between all parties at all times
16	Helping individual and group expertise bond into a creative working team
17	Promoting, encouraging and celebrating individual and group accomplishments at every stage
18	Pausing for democratic, informal and organised feedback on tasks and activities during their progress to completion and ensuring the results are acted on
19	Building in opportunities for further learning and development as activities progress
20	Promoting and presenting the results of individual and group achievement to internal and external stakeholders and leaders

NO.	AREA	RATING			
		1	2	3	4

Reviewing performance and working with performance problems – ensuring the best possible quality of outcomes from individual and group activity

21	Agreeing a schedule of review activity which enables all participants to contribute				
22	Collecting evaluation data, reviewing it with all participants and recording the results				
23	Arguing for change and development based on the evidence of evaluations				
24	Promoting a 'no blame' approach to solving individual and group performance problems				
25	Involving individuals and groups in supporting others who are encountering performance problems				
26	Providing opportunities to openly discuss individual and group differences				

Future visioning – promoting learning, development and strategy which meets current needs and looks beyond the horizon to the future

27	Promoting leading-edge research awareness of developments in individual and group fields of expertise				
28	Organising meetings to discuss future strategy and activity				
29	Providing incentives for developing shared and accessible banks of physical, people and financial resources				
30	Continuing to promote and celebrate success and support those performing less well				

but student numbers are declining, as are student retention and achievement. The students who participate in learning are mainly from the sections of society that traditionally participate, comprising a narrow range of social groups. The organisation needs to change its organisational culture to be able to remain viable, and to widen its participation amongst the community. In order to meet this challenge, the service at management level decided to:

- *Consult widely and fully* with staff about a changed vision and focus for the service. Results suggested staff recognised the changes were more in tune with the best traditions of adult education, and that a more organisation-wide approach to development and delivery would be most likely to achieve that, even if local centres lost some autonomy.

- *Set up agreed mechanisms for recording activity more clearly and analysing results* against agreed targets, which indicated reasons for course cancellations and drop-out, and led to measures which reduced both considerably.

- *Develop partnerships* with a wide range of voluntary organisations and others who had access to the target groups of students, and considerable educational experience of their own.

- *Provide support, guidance and coaching* for staff to help clarify roles and responsibilities, share good practice and contribute fully to making the changes work.

This approach to leadership by the organisation makes use of some of the distributed leadership strategies we have already discussed, and the adult education service is now much more effectively placed to meet the challenges of the future.

Cross-subject peer review

A medium-sized further education college had recently been inspected, and results in two of the curriculum areas had been mediocre. After discussion with all staff concerned, the innovative idea of *cross-subject peer review* was used to look at ways of improving by:

- *Creating peer review groups* comprising the two problem areas and two others from the college with a positive inspection profile, to link up and work together.

- *Agreeing clear terms of reference* for those groups in which all participants were seen as equal, and all curriculum areas shared practice through joint workshops and presentations.

- *Devolving responsibility to front-line teachers* to ensure there was no feeling of blame or guilt, but rather a shared goal of helping each other to improve.

- *Being open to change and listening to others* promoted reflection by all on apparent strengths and weaknesses, and sharing suggestions for improvement.

The results of this distribution of leadership were positive, with all participating staff developing a greater critical awareness of their own curriculum area, in addition to more understanding of curriculum areas they had little to do with before that point. Internal observations confirmed improvement in the problem areas, and the more successful areas identified and used a number of new aspects of learning technology as suggested to them by their colleagues. The experience radiated positive energy out to staff in other curriculum areas, who then started forming their own cross-subject peer review groups.

References

Learning and Skills Development Agency (2003) *LSRC Leading Learning Report Series: International Comparator Contexts*. London: Learning and Skills Research Centre.

Robinson, V. M. J., Lloyd, C. A. and Rowe, K. J. (2008) The impact of leadership on student outcomes: an analysis of the differential effects of leadership types. *Educational Administration Quarterly*, 44 (5): 635–674.

Robson, J. and Bailey, B. (2009) Bowing from the heart: an investigation into discourses of professionalism and the work of caring for students in further education. *British Educational Research Journal*, 35 (1): 99–117.

22

Becoming a reflective professional

This chapter introduces the idea of the 'reflective professional' in PCE, building on what we have so far described as being 'actively critical' by starting with some reflections on reflection itself. We continue by explaining what we mean by a 'reflective professional', and how you can draw on your own experience to grow as a teacher, and as a person. The chapter concludes by promoting the sense of support and shared professionalism which can be gained from joining with others in 'communities of practice'.

From the deep end to being a role model

The 2004 framework document on the future of teacher training in PCE argued that 'we want teachers in the learning and skills sector to become role models for lifelong learning' (Department for Education and Skills 2004: 5). One of the most positive definitions of lifelong learning, which we are happy to endorse, is from Aitcheson (2003), although he uses the term 'lifelong education', which he argues:

> is a comprehensive and visionary concept which includes formal, non-formal and informal learning extended throughout the lifespan of an individual to attain the fullest possible development in personal, social and vocational and professional life. . . . A key purpose of lifelong learning is democratic citizenship, connecting individuals and groups to the structures of social, political and economic activity.
>
> (Aitcheson, 2003: 165)

This definition is a powerful starting point, and the inclusion of all forms of learning, the personal, civic and social domains, is particularly welcome. Just what however is involved in teachers becoming 'role models' in this sense? Nesbit *et al.* (2004) write about 'great teachers' and argue that they:

> think strategically and act with commitment. When we watch these teachers we can see, and admire, their grasp of teaching technique. But these teachers have more than skill; they also think and act at a number of levels. Such teachers have a deep understanding of themselves and their students, and of the organisational

contexts in which they work. They think 'on their feet', and take a long term view of their work.

(Nesbit *et al.* 2004: 74)

We all want to become great teachers, don't we?

Critical reflection is an important part of that process.

Through the looking glass: analysing your experience using reflection

We all think or reflect about things. It is one of the most natural parts of everyone's lives. The learning wheel we have used in this book recognises the part reflection plays in learning, and Schon (1983) argued that reflection could help professionals to develop their practice. Schon saw practitioners as encountering many problems, grey areas and uncertainties in their work, and used the evocative phrase 'swampy lowlands' to describe those areas. Our own watery metaphor of the deep end presents a similar picture, and teachers in PCE can sometimes be surrounded by 'swampy lowlands' on all sides! Schon (1983) suggested professional practice could be developed through a spiral of action and reflection, whereby the practitioner acts, reflects on the action and plans new action, which is informed by the results of the reflection. The spiral is continuous, and can be interrupted and incomplete, and the reflection will not always solve problems. It could even cause problems. It does, however, help bring uncertainties to the surface, and provide a means of looking for solutions. This is the basis of *critical reflection*.

What is critical reflection?

'Without critical reflection, teaching will remain at best uninformed, and at worst ineffective, prejudiced and constraining' (Hillier 2002: xi). This fits nicely with the world view of this book, which recognises and embraces complexity and uncertainty, seeing them both as part of an opportunity to learn and develop. But can reflection really make a difference to what we do as teachers? Hillier (2002: 5) is confident that there are two 'main reasons' for using critical reflection:

- We can question our routine, convenient, everyday practices and ask ourselves about what really does and doesn't work.
- We can challenge some of our deeper, social and cultural thoughts, feelings and reactions, or what Hillier (2002: 7) calls our 'taken-for-granted assumptions'.

Consider these examples:

PowerPointless?

You have developed a really impressive set of PowerPoint slides for two of your courses, and have used a data projector regularly in your sessions to show the slides.

Every student who is present gets a set of handouts of the slides, and you place copies on the intranet so they are available for students outside class times. When you get student work in for assessment, you are a little disappointed to find that no one seems to make use of what is on the slides, and no one ever accesses them on the intranet. They seem to make much more use of the extracts from a TV sitcom which you used to illustrate bad practice.

Group activities rule!

You always include a range of group activities, collaborative tasks and projects in your teaching sessions, because you strongly believe your students both work and learn better this way. During the sessions there is almost always a good 'buzz', and the feedback from most students about the approach is positive. The achievement in the groups varies fairly widely, and is not better than another class where much more 'traditional' teaching is used.

Thinking point: how could critical reflection make a difference?

Both the examples above show teaching generally appearing to be working, and there is not a suggestion here that anything is seriously wrong. Look again at the situation and ask yourself just what 'routine, convenient, everyday practices' and 'taken-for-granted assumptions' are present. Try these challenging questions to get behind those practices and assumptions:

PowerPointless

- When I use PowerPoint in my teaching, what difference does it make and how do I know that?
- Why is the other resource more popular?
- Do I use PowerPoint mainly because I enjoy using it?
- What could I do instead?

Group activities

- Do I choose this style of teaching because I personally prefer it, or because it works better with and for my students?
- How would I react if I found out that 60 per cent of each session is taken up by 'teacher talk', that is, my own contributions to the session?
- How do I work with students who are uncomfortable with group work?

Critical reflection is about challenging and testing out what you do as a teacher, and being prepared to act on the results.

Using the DATA process

Hillier (2002) makes use of Peters's (1994) DATA process as a means of helping critical reflection, and it is well worth trying out. DATA is a problem-solving approach whose initials stand for *describe*, *analyse*, *theorise* and *act*, and the stages are:

- Describe the area of practice which you feel needs improvement or change.
- Analyse the factors contributing to the problem area of practice. You should dig deep here, and consider the assumptions and underlying beliefs and motives involved.
- Theorise possible ways to improve the practice, and suggest ways forward.
- Act on your theory, by trying out the new practice to see how it works (adapted from Hillier 2002).

Thinking point: trying DATA out

Think of an area of your teaching which you would like to reflect on more critically. It doesn't have to be a problem area, and indeed it may be a good idea to reflect on an area you feel is going very well. Use the DATA process to ask yourself questions about it. This can be carried out alongside formal evaluation procedures. Here are some suggestions:

- Keeping to time, and covering everything you need in your teaching sessions, is a constant problem. Why?
- You use group activity a lot of the time, but rarely give direct input to a group as a lecture or mini lecture. Why?
- You rarely use learning technology in your teaching. Why?

Work that area of practice through the DATA process, and see how the results work out.

The 'reflective professional' in PCE

We discussed the notion of 'capable' and 'extended' professionals earlier in the book. Is there an overall model of 'professionalism' which we can all aspire to and hope to develop in the current world of PCE? We want you all to be 'great teachers' in the ways described earlier in the chapter. We believe *reflective professionals* should:

- work inclusively with their students to assist them towards fulfilment of their life and career goals;
- develop and maintain mastery of their core teaching and specialist expertise;
- be actively critical;

- engage with the wider world of education and its communities of practice;
- work collaboratively with colleagues and students;
- develop and maintain their own personal vision;
- explore new knowledge, understanding, appreciation and practical application relating to teaching and learning;
- use their personal experience and professional development to seek to improve teaching and learning in PCE for the benefits of all involved.

Developing reflective professionals should be a central goal for PCE and all teachers should be striving for that goal.

Communities of practice

As you are grappling with the 'swampy lowlands', and even when teaching is calm and relaxed, it is highly likely that another teacher somewhere else is having the same, or at least a similar, experience. It may be a teacher in the session next door, or it may be someone in China. It could be happening now, or it may have happened years ago. Much as it's nice to feel you are unique, wouldn't it be helpful if that pool of experience and understanding could in some way be useful for you and for others? A positive approach to making use of our 'shared repertoire of communal resources' (Wenger 1998) is to become involved in 'communities of practice'.

A community of practice is a grouping of teaching professionals with shared interests, values and passions, who interact with each other on an ongoing basis.

The grouping can be small, face-to-face and local, or large, virtual and global, and it has a good chance of success if it follows three key principles:

- taking part should provide worthwhile experiences and understandings for each individual;
- taking part should provide worthwhile experiences and understandings for the community as a whole;
- the work of the community of practice may benefit the wider community of PCE.

At its best, a community of practice can be a major support to the idea of developing as a reflective professional, because it can highlight a number of factors, including:

- *You are not alone* – there are others who are experiencing the same successes and disasters.
- *You can push the frontiers forward* – others will want to work together on trying out something new.

- *Reinventing the wheel isn't compulsory* – if and when it has been done before, we can all make use of accumulated and shared experience.
- *Peers can review quality* – reviewing practice by and with your peers can be a powerful way of improving quality.

Strategy for survival: getting communities of practice to work

Drawing teachers together is not always helpful, and not all groupings would be communities of practice in our terms. If you try to follow these guidelines, however, you will give such a community a reasonable chance of success.

- All members need to know clearly what the grouping is for, and be able to develop and renegotiate that purpose, and participation, on an ongoing basis.
- Working together on shared tasks, responsibilities and projects can provide an active focus towards shared learning.
- Critical reflection and techniques such as the DATA process need to be built in to maintain focus, but don't overdo it.
- Where there is a social dimension to the community, this adds value, and can enhance the fun involved (it's often easy to forget about fun!).

Communities of practice in action

Two real examples of how communities of practice can work now follow.

Research into student support

A regional research network negotiated funding for a project to investigate models of student support in colleges, and how that affected retention rates. The network included practitioners from across PCE including further education and higher education. Individually, the participants had different specialist areas, working contexts and backgrounds, but their shared interest in student support drew them together on this occasion into a community of practice. As the project developed, the benefits of working in this way added considerable value, both to the experience of taking part in the research, and to the results for the individuals, the group as a whole and the wider field of student support. Innovative aspects of the projects and its benefits included:

- carrying out paired research interviews in which interviewers visited their paired partner's institution to carry out interviews;
- peer group reviewing and analysis of data prior to producing a final project report;
- collaborative presentation of results at regional and national conferences.

Developing an inter-institutional community of practice

Two South West land-based colleges combined forces to consider how to improve success rates on Level 3 provision. The action research project, funded by the SWitch Centre for Excellence in Teacher Training, addressed various different areas of teaching and learning and built a collaboration between staff at the two colleges. The components of the project included:

- joint analysis of benchmark data;
- agreement to focus on a small group of curriculum areas;
- adoption of key materials associated with developing 'expert learners' to be used by both colleges;
- visits by college staff to meet peers at the other college, and work in 'teaching pairs'.

The project developed several of the recognisable features of a community of practice, and the particular benefits of a mutually valued sharing of expertise and opportunities for networking were both commented on by participants as being particularly positive for them. The communities created are still surviving and moving forwards.

References

Aitcheson, J. (2003) Adult literacy and basic education: a SADC regional perspective. *Adult Education and Development*, 60: 161–171.

Department for Education and Skills (2004) *Equipping Our Teachers for the Future: Reforming Initial Teacher Training for the Learning and Skills Sector*. London: DfES.

Hillier, Y. (2002) *Reflective Teaching in Further and Adult Education*. London: Continuum.

Nesbit, T., Leach, L. and Foley, G. (2004) Teaching adults. In Foley, G. (ed.) *Dimensions of Learning: Adult Education and Training in a Global Era*. Maidenhead: Open University Press.

Peters, J. M. (1994) Instructors as researcher-and-theorists: faculty development in a community college. In Benn, R. and Fieldhouse, R. (eds) *Training and Professional Development in Adult and Community Education*. Exeter: CRCE.

Schon, D. (1983) *The Reflective Practitioner: How Professionals Think in Action*. New York: Basic Books.

Wenger, E. (1998) *Communities of Practice: Learning as a Social System* [Online] Communities of Practice: Best Practices [available at] http://www.co-i-l.com/coil/knowledge-garden/cop/lss.shtml (accessed 14 December 2009).

23

You can get involved in research and professional development

In Chapter 17 'opportunities worth taking' as a teacher were considered, and these were *projects*, *research*, *creating* and *externalling*. Each of those could in its own way be seen to involve aspects of what would be called 'research'. This chapter starts by considering what research is in PCE, and whether there really is a time and place for research, when you are so busy with so many other things. We strongly argue that research is not just worth making time for, but is essential if teachers and the PCE community are going to move forward to a positive future. Examples of research, and where it has made a difference, are provided, combined with guidance on the approaches, values and skills needed to carry out meaningful and developmental research. Professional development is then introduced as a means of keeping you in touch with the 'leading edge' of your own specialist area, and as a way of refreshing your teaching. We close the chapter with an appeal to 'get nerdy' by following and maintaining your own research and professional development passions.

What is research?

Many of the debates around research centre on these themes and questions:

- 'The truth is out there'. If you look hard enough you can find it.
- 'Life, the universe and everything' are all full of uncertainty in a rapidly changing world, so can truth really be found?
- Does research have to have 'impact' to be worth doing?
- Is any research genuinely objective?

Discoveries are being made now almost every year which would have been considered impossible only a few years ago. Feelings of uncertainty about research and truth are only to be expected in such an environment. In addition, the working environment of PCE has often been seen over the last three decades as lacking a 'research focus' and in particular a 'research culture' (Hayes 2003: 155). One reason this is the case is uncertainty about the results of research. As Lea (2003: 143) puts it, 'the **k**... research concern here is the increasing difficulty we now all have in claiming ther is a Mount Olympus from which we can observe educational reality'. It could therefore be seen by pressured teachers, and in particular their managers, that giving time, resources and priority to research is difficult to justify.

> Uncertainty about 'educational reality' does not, however, mean we shouldn't even try to look for it.

We agree wholeheartedly with the powerful assertion that 'all researchers should seek to advance knowledge and truth' (Hayes 2003: 15). Moving understanding of what we do forward and investigating and questioning policy, principles and practice is surely essential for us all.

How then can we define research? Drawing on Robson (1997), our definition is:

> Principled enquiry to help us gain an understanding of the human world of PCE, which can contribute to new knowledge and understanding, and which can inform change and development.

The benefits of research

When a teacher's time is already full up to the point when 24 hours often isn't enough, wouldn't getting involved in research add to that pressure? In some ways of course that may be the case, as research does take time and effort, but it does at its best offer real rewards, including:

- You will develop new insights, ideas, materials and skills which will enhance your teaching.
- Taking time to read and 'be critical' about writing and literature through research (especially struggling through the most pretentious writing you will ever encounter) can be a great way of energising your thinking and actions.
- Research credits on your CV can be extremely helpful.
- You will develop a more 'leading edge' understanding of your specialist area.
- Your capacity to be 'actively critical' will be improved.
- When the next new initiative is about to be implemented in your organisation, you may well be able to make a strong case for how it should (or shouldn't) be introduced.

Making sense of research: lit from different angles

Research is rarely, if ever, genuinely objective, which needs to be kept very much to the fore when both using it and doing it. This can be illustrated with an image from film or TV. If you wish to change how your audience views the subject, changing the lighting can be a powerful and effective way of doing that, without changing the subject at all. If for instance you light a human face from the both sides with diffused soft light, it normally enhances the natural features of that face in a way which most people would feel is warm and positive. If you light the same face solely with strong concentrated light from immediately below, perhaps coloured red, it will look harsh and probably scary. In research terms, if a piece of research is being funded by a government, organisation or company, isn't it at least possible that they will want to see the results 'lit' in a way which will agree with their ideas, or show them in a favourable light? If a researcher is investigating the retention of their own students, wouldn't they want the results to be seen in the best light for them? When doing research we need therefore to:

- acknowledge the effect which factors such as opinions, values, circumstances and previous research have on research and the research process;
- take account of those factors when planning, carrying out and writing up research.

Research strategies and skills

If you are going to make the most of opportunities to do research, these are strategies you should adopt, and skills you will need to develop:

- *Be clear about what you are trying to find out and why* – devise clear questions you intend to ask, which relate to the problem you are looking to solve. This doesn't necessarily mean you will effortlessly advance through the research to clear and useful results, but it will start you off in the right direction.

- *Get training* – research skills at one level can be straightforward, but in many ways are sophisticated and complex. Training in skills such as developing research ideas, questions and projects, research methods, data collection and analysis techniques, reviewing literature and disseminating and publishing results should be available through your employer or other local learning providers. Take advantage of that training as you will find you often use it.

- *Get access and permission* – in simple terms, when researching anyone, or anything, you will need on most occasions to get *permission* of some sort, and to make sure the subjects of your research will be there when you want to research them (*access*). At its simplest level this will involve asking perhaps your own students, and at its most complex submitting a proposal to a research and/or ethics committee, which may only meet twice a year. If the subjects aren't there, or you haven't got permission, your research will not get very far.

- *Choose your research methods carefully* – there are many methods available to use in research including interviews, questionnaires and observation. Select and justify appropriate methods.

- *Don't forget the ethics* – research is carried out mainly by people on people, so the way in which you carry it out should take account of that fact. As the British Educational Research Association (2004: 4) indicates, this is about reaching 'an ethically acceptable position in which their [researchers'] actions are considered justifiable and sound'.

- *Treat other research/writing critically* – bearing in mind what we said about research being 'lit from different angles', ask questions of other research (and your own) including: Should I take this research at face value? Do the results stand up to scrutiny? Did the methods seem appropriate?

- *Find out where your research fits* – there is very little in education which hasn't already had some research done on or about it. Finding out what has been done before is really important, as it can guide and inform your own research. Information skills are very important here, as massive numbers of research publications are now available electronically.

- *Always expect the unexpected* – it's surprising how often in doing research things don't work out exactly as planned. Just like the rest of life, really! This can range from exciting unexpected outcomes to arriving for a set of interviews and finding no one there. Just be ready for it.

- *Be confident about what you have researched and the results* – part of the benefit of doing research is that it builds your own confidence about the topic of that research. Be prepared to stand up for that confidence in your role as a teacher. (If you have followed our guidance your research should stand up to scrutiny.)

Thinking point: your own research project

Taking account of what we have covered so far in this chapter, think of an area of your teaching work which you consider to be a problem and try to create a 'research question' about it such as 'Why do my students always want to sit in the same place in the class?' or 'What is the current thinking on the benefits or disadvantages of using a virtual learning environment?'

Planning and carrying out a piece of research which could help you to answer either question could be undertaken by:

- thinking through what topics and issues may come up when trying to answer the question;
- finding out the 'state of knowledge' in this area from existing research;
- considering which methods would help you collect data for the research;
- deciding on when, where and how you could do the research.

Now you've worked through this, go ahead and get researching!

Research making a difference

We would argue that research doesn't always have to have obvious impact, or to change things, or to show clear results, as it will still make a contribution in other ways. There are, however, many times when it can make a real difference, as these two examples show.

Reasons for dropping out

During the late 1990s, drop-out of students from courses, particularly in further education colleges, was still at a relatively high level. The main way of judging why that was the case was to take the official figures of retention for any course (e.g. 20 started and 15 finished, hence retention of 80 per cent), and to rate them across the organisation. Those figures were then compared with figures from similar courses in different organisations, and target figures set for retention for most organisations. If a course did not fare well using those measures, it was seen as reflecting on the quality of the provision and the learning. Research carried out by Bloomer and Hodkinson (1999; Hodkinson and Bloomer 2001) involved interviewing a large number of students about what made them more likely to drop out. This showed that those reasons were complicated and varied, and often involved circumstances which were nothing at all to do with the college or its teaching. The key difference which this research made was not necessarily to dramatically change the way things were done, but to shift the emphasis away from counting retention figures, and towards providing more effective support for students. For the teacher on the ground it wasn't a huge revelation, but it did contribute to the development of a greater range of support services which they could draw on for the benefit of their students. It added significantly to our understanding of why students drop out, even if it didn't provide a complete solution.

Listening to disabled students

An adult and community learning (ACL) service in a semi-rural area had a recorded disabled population of 19 per cent, but only 6 per cent of current ACL students had declared a disability. The team of tutors, organisers and student representatives wished to both find out what lay behind the figures, and work towards increasing that participation figure. They got together as a group, including two of their existing disabled students, to help produce a small research project. A postal survey was carried out of students declaring a disability over the last three years, and meetings set up at three centres. The meetings were held as facilitated student-only discussion/focus groups, and a wide-ranging discussion resulted about many issues. The results included:

- Much information emerged which was used to develop plans for future provision.
- User groups were set up for disabled students.
- Plans to improve access and resources for disabled users could be more effectively prioritised.
- Disabled students felt valued and their confidence improved.
- The service organisers recognised this approach could be beneficial in other ways such as establishing tutor user groups.

Professional development or 'reflective professionals don't stand still'

A total of 30 hours per year of continuing professional development for teachers in PCE is now compulsory (Department for Education and Skills 2007). We would suggest CPD should be continuous, starting with initial training, and continuing throughout the professional life of a teacher. Such an official endorsement of CPD is welcome, but just what is continuing professional development?

Continuing professional development is the process which helps teachers to develop as practitioners, as students and as part of the community of practice of PCE.

CPD can serve a number of purposes, but at its best it can keep us moving forward as 'reflective professionals', be energising and promote innovation. It can also help us greatly in assisting us to develop and extend our capacity to work effectively with our students. We are always going to be busy, but we shouldn't stand still, and we would hope that the requirement for CPD will make it a genuine entitlement for all teachers.

The learning curve: guiding values of professional development

The Institute for Learning (IfL) is the professional organisation for teaching staff in PCE. It promotes a worthwhile vision of 'high performing teaching and training professionals, self-regulating and self-improving through their commitment to continuing professional development (CPD)' (Institute for Learning 2009: 2). It goes on to suggest that:

CPD gives the public, learners, the teaching community and the sector confidence that teachers, trainers, tutors and assessors are continuously improving their skills, knowledge and expertise. CPD is the hallmark of the professional.

(Institute for Learning 2009: 2)

There is also a very useful set of values produced by the Staff and Educational Development Association (SEDA) which it indicates underpin all its activity. These contain an extra aspirational dimension to professional development for teachers which doesn't emerge as strongly from the IfL vision. SEDA suggests professional development should contribute to:

1 *An understanding of how people learn*. Learning is a complex and challenging business that takes place in different ways, in different contexts. Many factors encourage or inhibit learning and these will vary from learner to learner, depending upon purpose and environment.

2 *Scholarship, professionalism and ethical practice*. Scholarship, professionalism and ethical practice are inextricably linked and underpin our work.

3 *Working in and developing learning communities*. There are many kinds of learning communities.

4   *Working effectively with diversity and promoting inclusivity*. In our learning support and development practice it is important to identify and seek to meet the many and varied learning needs of the learners with whom we work. In doing so we offer opportunities for us and for our learners to learn from, and also, where appropriate, to learn about each other.

5   *Continuing reflection on professional practice*. As professionals, we need to continue to learn and to develop our professional expertise. Perhaps the most powerful tool for supporting our development is our continuing scholarly, deep, analytic reflection on our practice.

6   *Developing people and processes*. In our learning support and development practice we are concerned with the development of ourselves, our learners, the institutions we work in and the educational processes with which we work (adapted from SEDA 2003).

Thinking point: does my professional development match up?

■   List any activities you have undertaken in the last six months which you would consider to be continuing professional development.

■   Using the 'learning curve' values in the previous section, check off how many of them were addressed by that CPD.

■   Are there areas which are consistently covered or not covered when you undertake CPD?

Well done, you've just completed what may be your first ever *Professional Development Record*.

Strategy for survival: planning ahead for CPD

■   If you have learnt something new and valuable from your own CPD, offer to share it with others to enhance theirs.

■   Based on the results of the last thinking point, plan out what you'll be looking for in CPD for the next six months, and what you'll be avoiding.

■   If there are obvious and continuing gaps, raise it with your team, your department and your boss.

Get nerdy!

At times, it is possible for professional development to get linked up with appraisal, professional formation and a number of other formal and organisational expectations and requirements. Although this is often an important part of developing as a teacher, and provides accountability for development which may have cost a great deal of time and money, it can at times lead one to forget that learning should be fulfilling and fun. With that in mind we would encourage you all to 'get nerdy'. Most of us hav our deep interests and passions which we find completely absorbing and interesting. For some it may be the history of the British monarchy, for others restoring vintage cars, for others trekking in Peru and for others music in the 1970s. One thing about these passions is that we cannot be sure that our colleagues, friends and family will share them. Hence terms such as 'anorak', 'geek' and 'nerd'. What they do, however, is illustrate just how important such passions are in our lives, and how powerful getting involved in what are essentially personal learning activities can be. As this book draws to a close, we wish to promote the notion that to 'get nerdy' is a good thing. We would like it to be about teaching and learning but, if not, just think of this:

If your students end up as absorbed in what you have to teach them as you have been by getting nerdy, you must now be out of the 'deep end'.

The 'get nerdy' challenge

This is the one of the ultimate tests of a teacher.

- Get together a group of your students, colleagues, friends or family.
- Prepare a short teaching session on any subject which gets you nerdy.
- The aim of the session is to develop or change the views of the group on your passion.
- Run the session and start by asking the group's current view.
- Ask the same question at the end.

If the views have become more positive you can now call yourself a professional teacher!

References

Bloomer, M. and Hodkinson, P. (1999) *College Life: The Voice of the Student*. London: FEDA.

British Educational Research Association (2004) *Revised Ethical Guidelines for Educational Research*. Southwell, Notts: BERA.

Department for Education and Skills (2007) *The Further Education Teachers' Continuing Professional Development and Registration (England) Regulations 2007*. London: DfES.

Hayes, D. (2003) The truth about educational research. In Lea, J., Hayes, D., Armitage, A., Lomas, L. and Markless, S. *Working in Post-Compulsory Education*. Maidenhead: Open University Press.

Hodkinson, P. and Bloomer, M. (2001) Dropping out of further education: complex causes and simplistic policy assumptions. *Research Papers in Education* 16: 117–140.

Institute for Learning (2009) *Guidelines for Your Professional Development*. London: IfL.

Lea, J. (2003) Overview: conducting research in educational settings. In Lea, J., Hayes, D., Armitage, A., Lomas, L. and Markless, S. *Working in Post-Compulsory Education*. Maidenhead: Open University Press.

Robson, C. (1997) *Real World Research: A Resource for Social Scientists and Practitioner Researchers*. Oxford: Blackwell.

SEDA (2003) [Online] *SEDAs Values: Further Guidance* [available at:] http://www.seda.ac.uk/about.html?p=2_1_1 (accessed 14 January 2010).

24

Future gazing

Where and what next?

This chapter closes the book by drawing together several key themes. We first take stock of where PCE is situated now in the overall picture of UK education, and conclude that the second decade of the twenty-first century is going to be a momentous time for the sector. We gaze into two possible futures for PCE, one grey and gloomy, and one positive and energising, and make a plea for steps to be taken to leave the grey behind and head for the positive. The book closes with a final call to all teachers in PCE to work together towards that more positive future, and the final 'out of the deep end test' just to make sure you are now able to swim confidently off towards the sun setting on the horizon.

Where are we now?

Two documents published in the second half of 2009 just about sum up the state of PCE at present. The first is *Skills for Growth: The National Skills Strategy*, published in November 2009. Here are two selected statements from that document.

> As we emerge from the banking crisis and rebuild the British economy, the skills system needs a stronger focus towards strategic skills, businesses need to contribute more to shaping demand for skills, and learners need to be able to choose where they train and what they study to drive competition and improve courses.
>
> (BIS 2009: 5)

> The goal of this strategy is a skills system defined not simply by targets based on achieved qualifications, but by 'real world' outcomes.
>
> (BIS 2009: 5)

Second, a publication with the terrifying title of *Getting More for Less: Efficiency in the Public Sector* by the think tank Demos.

> The current climate offers a real opportunity to transform the way services are delivered. The savings on offer from focusing on providing effective services might take a while to accumulate – and in some cases might even result in extra initial

costs. But, counter-intuitively, the size and scale of the cuts that are coming in public spending offer an opportunity to think in the long term. To invest now in projects that make long-term savings suddenly makes more sense when public spending deficits will not be cleared for a decade.

So start with effectiveness – get things right. Efficiency will follow.

(Bartlett 2009: 8–9)

We will now compare these statements with some words from the past. First:

Learning is the key to prosperity – for each of us as individuals, as well as for the nation as a whole. Investment in human capital will be the foundation of success in the knowledge-based global economy of the twenty-first century. This is why the Government has put learning at the heart of its ambition.

(DfES 1998: foreword)

This quote is from a government green paper on lifelong learning called *The Learning Age* published in 1998.

Second:

Through this gloom the [XXXX] has brightly coupled its vast wealth and manpower to indigent industry and importunate further education, bringing forth several generations of training and/or work experience schemes for both jobless youth and those in jobs without training.

. . . all young people of sixteen–eighteen years of age who have no job or who are not engaged in further or higher education should have the opportunity of training, of participation in a job creation programme, or of work experience.

(Edwards 1984: 24)

This quote is about the Manpower Services Commission, a government organisation which started operation in 1974, and which was one of many initiatives and organisations which impacted on PCE.

Comparison and analysis of these words and the context of the time could take up a great deal of effort, but the key points we would wish to make are:

- Publications by or for politicians tend to use language which sounds impressive, but which generally fails to communicate the practicalities and application of policies effectively.

- Approaches to education, and in particular to PCE, tend to go in cycles, and repeat themselves on a worryingly regular basis.

- Working in PCE for five years or more tends to make you ask what has been learnt by the sector during the previous five years!

The best way to make sense of these types of statement is probably to consider them as 'the vision' which is laid out for us by others, and 'the reality' as how this vision is experienced in practice.

As a teacher you will often agree with the vision, but what you will be faced with is the reality.

PCE is a sector which manages to get much of what it does right, whilst at the same time (and probably in the same organisation) getting much wrong.

Where do we go from here?

Professor David Hicks, in his excellent book *Lessons for the Future* (2002), provides an insightful consideration of the place of the future in our education system. His genuinely aspirational view of the future states:

> The future is an integral part of everyday life. We spend a large part of our time thinking about it. Identifying goals for the future enhances our capacity to work in the present, adds to our motivation and helps give us direction. While on the one hand the future is intangible, it is also of crucial importance. Human existence cannot be conceived without it.
>
> Hicks (2002: 14)

He presents a convincing argument for the curriculum to 'ask the question: where are we going and where do we want to go, locally, nationally and globally' (Hicks 2002: 14).

One of the central purposes of this book is to help you survive the present but not to forget the future.

To conclude our journey, we will ask you to carefully reflect on some aspects of what the future could hold and encourage you as a teacher to 'promote the knowledge, skills and understanding needed to live responsibly in a multicultural society and an independent world' (Hicks 2002: 128).

Two visions of the future

In some respects, prospects for PCE are problematic and difficult. Many of the pressures we face can appear immovable and difficult to resolve and, as we have said, the sector is diverse, and in some ways not united. The future could lead in two different directions.

Grey and gloomy

Imagine this start to a working day.

8.00   After some difficulty getting access to the building, because of a new security system, you arrive at your desk (in an open-plan shared space with 12 others) as usual, and start to check your emails. Only 90 unanswered today, which is quite an improvement on yesterday.

8.30   The 25 most urgent emails are answered. Over 250 still in the inbox. Join the queue by the photocopier to copy handouts to use in your 9.00 session. It ran out of paper 15 minutes ago, and your department has exceeded its monthly limit. Collect your memory stick with all the electronic materials for the day and head for session 1.

9.00   At the start of the diploma session 10 of your group of 18 students are present. The rest arrive in ones and twos over the next 30 minutes, delayed by the new security system, which wouldn't let them in either to start with. Your PowerPoint slides crash after the second slide, but no technician is available to sort it out for 40 minutes as they have had their hours reduced as part of the efficiency measures. One of your students manages to sort the problem out, by which time the session has only five minutes left.

10.00 Your students go out into the learning centre to work independently on their assignments, and you return to your desk to finalise your plan for the next session, in which you are being observed by the consultant appointed to pre-inspect your organisation.

10.45 After speaking to the eighth student to come to your desk you do manage to complete the plans for the session, and arrive only to discover your observer has already been there for 10 minutes. The session goes really well, and the observer rushes off to his next session saying 'see you at the feedback session at 6.00 this evening'. He is doing eight in a day, and is expensive to employ, so he is holding feedback sessions at the end of the day, which staff have to attend.

12.00 Start your 30-minute lunch break.

12.25 Eat a bought sandwich and gulp a cold coffee after six interruptions of various kinds to your break.

12.30 Course team meeting with six others. Agenda item 1, 'Improving retention', takes up all the time, and the item you were going to give, 'Imaginative uses of PowerPoint', is postponed for the fourth time.

13.30 Meeting with your head of department, at which he asks 'How's the teacher training course going?' and mentions he's not sure if there's enough money to renew your short-term contract at the end of the year. You answer that you are really enjoying the course but haven't made the last two sessions, as you have been covering for staff sickness. You explain you will need to start looking for other work.

Need we continue?

Although the scenario above is exaggerated, all the elements which make it up are present in PCE today. Things could go in that direction.

Positive and energising

We'll call David Hicks to our assistance again, as he suggests three key questions to ask, which can help to develop ideas and plans for the future which can be both personalised and collective.

Where are we now?

ON THE POSITIVE SIDE

- We work in a sector which has a record of embracing diversity, facing and introducing massive change rapidly, and to a major degree successfully.
- We have opportunities to make positive uses of inclusive approaches, learning technology and a flexible curriculum, for the benefit of all.
- Significant improvements to buildings and facilities have been made, with the prospect of more in the future.
- Opportunities for initial training and professional development are likely to increase significantly in the near future.
- In order to meet the expectations and targets set by government, the workforce needs to grow.

ON THE NEGATIVE SIDE

- Teachers in PCE are paid less than other teachers and their conditions of employment are worse than for any other teachers.
- The global financial situation has left many organisations facing an uncertain future.
- A number of serious issues need to be addressed about quality in PCE.

Where do we want to go?

- Towards a better trained and qualified workforce.
- To a situation in which PCE is flexible for both the students and the teachers.
- To a situation in which teachers are consulted, and their views both listened to and acted on, at all levels, local, national and international.
- Making use of the capacity of learning technology to connect, administer and facilitate interaction, and to genuinely reduce the paper mountain.
- A rationalisation of our labyrinthine qualifications framework into a clearer, more transparent system.
- Towards a situation with more leadership and less management.
- To the recognition that teachers are people too.

How do we get there?

- Teachers have to be better paid, and have reduced workloads.

- Developing and supporting communities of practice for teachers, and communities of learning for students, needs to move to centre stage.

- Providers should be funded for more long-term security but expected to meet clear goals and objectives over a longer period.

- Teachers should all be provided with an entitlement to supervision, mentoring, initial training and professional development, and the time and resources to make the most of it.

- Governments and other key stakeholders need to show trust in teachers that they can get it right.

Thinking point and strategy for future survival

Using the same questions, look into your future, and commit yourself to work towards it with enthusiasm.

The out of the deep end test

Given the title of this book, we have to insist on asking you some testing questions at the end to see if the mission has been worthwhile. The change from being 'in at the deep end' to swimming confidently towards the setting sun may well have been quite a journey, and you may not yet be all the way there. If you can answer most of these questions with a positive, we can officially recognise you as now *out of the deep end*.

- Does the prospect of your next month of work fill you with dread or excitement?

- When you are working with your students can you handle the majority of situations which may arise, both expected and unexpected?

- Can you remember a growing group of students for whom you have made a difference?

- Are you regularly involved in research and professional development activities?

- Can you effectively stand up for yourself in contact with managers, peers and others?

- Do you make sure you reflect critically on your work and actively seek to improve it?

- Has your specialist area grown in depth and substance?

- Do you work with others to develop communities of practice?

- Are you proud of your job, yourself and the work you do?

You should be, especially if you remember what we said at the start of the book.

You may or may not feel that education can change the world, but there is no doubt that at some stage, and if you're both lucky and good at your job, you will often help to change someone else's world and life for the better.

References

Bartlett, J. (2009) *Getting More for Less: Efficiency in the Public Sector*. London: Demos.

BIS (2009) *Skills for Growth: The National Skills Strategy. Executive Summary*. London: Department for Business, Skills and Innovation.

DfES (1998) *The Learning Age: A Renaissance for a New Britain*. London: Department for Education and Skills.

Edwards, T. (1984) *The Youth Training Scheme: A New Curriculum*. London: Falmer Press.

Hicks, D. (2002) *Lessons for the Future: The Missing Dimension in Education*. London: Routledge Falmer.

Glossary

Achievement   The learning which students complete, usually in terms of qualifications gained.

Additional learning needs   Needs which learners have, which are likely to mean they will require extra support to achieve their learning goals. Examples are a disability or a learning difficulty.

Aim   A goal which will result in learning.

Attainment   The achievements and accomplishments of our students.

Awarding body   One of the organisations which offer qualifications for learning providers to use with their students. They include City and Guilds, EdExcel and others.

Benchmark   A standard against which an item can be judged against other similar items.

Civil society   A term used to describe the goal of an inclusive, socially cohesive society which recognises and values diversity and works towards achieving a sense of community.

Community of practice   A grouping of professionals with a shared field of interest, who interact with each other as a group.

Curriculum areas   The collection of similar subjects which make up a reasonably discrete area of provision, for example business and management.

Differentiation   Actively planning learning activity to take account of the differences between students.

Functional skills   Practical skills in English, mathematics, and information and communication technology (ICT) for young people up to 19.

Hot desking   The practice of providing staff with a group of desks which they use on a 'first come first served basis'. Whoever is in uses whichever desk is available.

Inclusivity   An approach to teaching which takes account of, and makes adjustments to include, all students at all times.

Individual learning plans (ILPs)   Plans for individual learners which describe and track their progress in learning and achievement over time.

Induction   A structured period of activities to help new employees to settle in and function effectively during the first stage of a new job.

Information literacy   Knowledge of one's information concerns and needs, and the ability to identify, locate, evaluate, organise and effectively create, use and communicate information to address issues or problems at hand.

Initial assessment   Tests, tasks or activities which students or potential students work through, to assist with matching their learning programme to their own needs.

Initial teacher training   The mandatory programme of training for a teacher in PCE, which leads to being a qualified teacher.

Intranet   A network of computers, usually within one organisation, and used by that organisation.

Knowledge society   A term representing the combination of technology, progress and development which should enable society to move forward.

Learning centre A location, normally in a local community, where learning opportunities are available to that community, often primarily in computer or online courses.

Learning champion A worker or volunteer who has an official role in promoting learning in an organisation.

Learning experience Any experience from which learning can take place.

Learning site Any location at which learning takes place.

Learning styles and preferences The different ways in which a particular individual may prefer to learn, such as through 'hands on' or through 'visual' approaches.

Needs analysis A variety of approaches, procedures and activities which can be used to identify particular learning or other needs.

Objective A statement indicating what learning will take place.

Online Using the Internet and other forms of electronic communication.

Open access Courses or centres where students or potential students can drop in or book in at times when they wish to learn.

Personalisation Tailoring learning to the needs of an individual.

Profiling Gathering information about aspects of a person to help understand them better.

Retention Keeping the amount of drop-out from your courses to an absolute minimum.

Risk assessment A procedure for checking the hazards in your teaching spaces, and considering the risk of accidents taking place.

Scheme of work A detailed outline of a learning programme including objectives, content, resources, learning activity, assessment and evaluation, and details of inclusive approaches and differentiation.

Skills for life The term for learning which helps adults improve their literacy, language or numeracy.

Specification document The full details of a qualification including detailed content, assessment, quality assurance and centre information.

Sustainable development Development that meets the needs of the present without compromising the ability of future generations to meet their own needs.

Tutorial Times when a teacher works directly with one or more students to discuss and review aspects of their learning or related matters.

Index